riting books

Writing
Successful
Textbooks

Writing Handbooks

Writing Successful Textbooks

Anthony Haynes

A & C Black • London

To Karen, Frances, Jonty and Simon

First published 2001
A & C Black (Publishers) Limited
37 Soho Square, London W1D 3QZ

© 2001 Anthony Haynes

ISBN 0–7136–5734–0

A CIP catalogue record for this book is available
from the British Library.

Typeset in 10½ on 12½ pt Sabon
Printed and bound in Great Britain by
Creative Print and Design (Wales), Ebbw Vale

Contents

Acknowledgements

My thanks to: the staff at A & C Black, especially Tesni Hollands for commissioning the book and providing constructive comment; Fiona Wilson for her comments on the manuscript; Brenda Stones for her expert advice on schools publishing; Sarah McNamara for permission to quote from her book proposal; and Yvonne Hillier for permission to use her book proposal in the appendix.

Most of all, I would like to thank Michelle 'Whisky' Looknanan for having read and criticised the entire manuscript. Any weaknesses that remain are surely Whisky's responsibility.

I have drawn a good deal on my experience of working as a commissioning editor for the Continuum International Publishing Group. The views expressed here, however, are my own and not necessarily those of my employer.

Foreword

Congratulations. The fact that you have bought this book sets you apart from most people contemplating turning their lecture notes and course material into a textbook. How natural a well-written textbook looks at first glance. How easy it appears to translate notes into whole chapters and thence into a complete book with a consistent style and rhythm. But it is not an easy task. This slim handbook will guide you through the necessary steps, the tricks and tips to aid readability, structure, style and presentation. In short a well-crafted textbook that meets the specific needs of a defined audience of students and lecturers. You will come to appreciate the self-discipline required to plan and deliver the manuscript in time to meet a narrow publication window. A hard won self-discipline to snatch the odd hour between lecturing, core research and the other demands of modern academic life. Perhaps the discipline to work while your colleagues are relaxing on holiday.

And why should I care? I must confess to having a vested interest. Blackwell Retail is best known for its flagship book shop in Oxford that caters for the needs of a far wider audience than the academics and students of the Oxford colleges. But our bread and butter is the sale of textbooks to the thousands of students who visit our campus branches up and down the country. In our experience, it requires more than an entry on a reading list to sell a textbook. The student grapevine is a powerful medium for influencing the purchase decisions of their peer group. Simplicity, clarity and the ability to put across complex new ideas while under pressure win many friends late in the evening the night before a lecture or essay deadline.

Philip Blackwell, Chief Executive, Blackwell's

Part One: Preparation

1. Authorship

Picture yourself a few years from now. Your second textbook has just been published – the one which your publisher invited you to write after the success of your first. You will start work on the second edition of your first book when you return from the holiday (paid for, of course, either by your royalties or the work that has come your way as a result of publication). You have a sense of well-being: perhaps, if you teach in some way, it's because your work has become so much easier now that your notes and handouts are in book form and your students recognise that you're an authority on your subject – or perhaps it's simply that you have the satisfaction of knowing that thousands of students have come to understand things that would have been beyond them without your book.

Of course, this is a particularly rosy scenario. Not all textbook authors – even successful ones – achieve all of the aspects of success mentioned in this vision. On the other hand, none of these elements is unheard of or even particularly rare. And, in fact, authors of textbooks sometimes achieve more than this. One American author claimed to run his private aeroplane on the proceeds of his textbook on economics. Textbook authorship might not be as glamorous as some of the forms of writing covered by this series – there is no Nobel prize available for writing a textbook, nor do textbooks get made into Hollywood films – but it does have its rewards.

The purpose of this book is simply to help you write a textbook, get it published, and make a success of it. The idea for the book grew out of my experience as a commissioning (or acquisitions) editor for an international publishing house. Most of the books that I commission are textbooks aimed at school, university or professional markets. I work with the whole gamut of authors, from the previously unpublished to the experienced and highly successful. Through working with inexperienced authors, I have seen how difficult it can be to write a good textbook. I like to ensure that they don't have to learn by trial and error. Instead, I try to pass on the lessons that I have learnt from my experienced authors. Frequently I have found myself thinking, 'If only there were a book that I could recommend – a book that would take the mystery out of the process.' *Writing Successful Textbooks* is that book.

There is no great secret about what makes a good textbook. I have often asked people what they have valued about the best textbooks they have read. Their answers have been almost boringly predictable. Good textbooks are:

Authoritative
Comprehensive
Pitched at the right level
Clear
Organised
Up to date

And that's about it. In contrast to some forms of writing – poetry, for example – the mystery lies not at all in the qualities that define the finished product, but wholly in the question of how you, as the author, get to that finished product. This book will demystify that process.

As a glance back at the above list will confirm, much of the secret of successful textbook writing is linguistic. That is, it is a matter of how to use words accurately, link passages clearly and so on. Part Two of this book deals with such issues. This chapter, however, is rather different. Instead of focusing on the writing itself, it focuses on you – you as an author. Its aim is to explain what characterises successful textbook authors and to show how you can assess yourself as a prospective textbook writer.

What characterises successful textbook authors?

Look back at the list of characteristics of successful textbooks. Some of the qualities required of authors may be inferred directly from that list. The demands that a textbook be authoritative and comprehensive, for example, imply that the author must have sound knowledge and understanding of his or her field. That might sound obvious, but it is worth probing further. Just how much knowledge and understanding is required?

The answer has two dimensions: depth and breadth. So far as the former is concerned, the author's knowledge and understanding must be sufficiently advanced and secure to ensure that his or her textbook *is* accurate and reliable and is *not* misleading for the level that the book's readers are working towards. The last few words of the previous sentence are crucial. They explain why it is that the author of a textbook need not be an expert in his or her field (if by 'expert' we mean somebody working at a subject's cutting edge).

Indeed, experts often fail to make good writers of textbooks. As I write, one of the textbooks I have commissioned is two years overdue. I will probably cancel the author's contract. The problem is not that the author is insufficiently expert. On the contrary, his previous book in my list – a work of original scholarship, not a textbook – won the most prestigious prize available to writers in his field. The problem is rather that he is *too* expert: he is so aware of the complexity and nuances of his subject that he finds it impossible to write down to the level at which his readers are working.

An author's knowledge, then, need be only so deep. The same does not apply to breadth of knowledge. To be successful, a textbook needs to be comprehensive. Most purchasers of textbooks want to buy a 'one stop' resource that will cover their entire course. Authors, therefore, need to know and understand *all* of the topics on all of the syllabuses followed by its target audience.

Overall, the knowledge profile of a textbook author at the beginning of a textbook project is usually as follows. He or she:

- is familiar with most of the subject matter to be covered
- has less familiarity with – and therefore a need to revise – a minority of topics
- is unfamiliar with a few awkward corners of the subject – usually those that feature on only a few syllabuses or have come to prominence only recently

By the end of the authorship process I find that writers are often not only familiar with all of the relevant subject matter, but also have retained it all in their heads. Fortunately the latter feat is not obligatory.

So far we have discussed only knowledge of subject matter. An author also requires knowledge of the *context* in which the textbook will be used. It is essential to have thorough knowledge of the courses on which a textbook might be studied. A minimum requirement is to know the syllabuses, including any changes that are in the pipeline, and the adoption guidelines or standards for your subject.

In the US, for example, more than twenty states publish adoption policies stating what features they consider desirable for school textbooks. In addition, several subject associations propose national standards for teaching and learning in their areas of the curriculum. In the UK there are national curricula or guidelines and, within their frameworks, examination board syllabuses.

The importance of this kind of knowledge can be seen from the success of one British textbook written for students learning to work with children. The book is neither well written nor well edited – and yet it is a market leader. It sells thousands of copies year after year and is one of its publisher's most lucrative books. The reason for its success is simply that its contents correspond much more closely to the national day-care standards – and therefore the syllabuses that prepare students to meet those standards – than any of its competitors.

It is helpful too to know the structure of the courses through which students follow those syllabuses. How long do they last? What shape do they take? In what order do students encounter the various components of their syllabus? Such factors help to determine what students will require from the textbooks they use.

The value of such knowledge is illustrated by a textbook called *Essential GCSE English for Mature Students*. This book was published for what in England and Wales is known as the GCSE market. GCSE is an examination that is usually taken by 16 year olds. The publishers (Collins Educational) noticed, however, that a number of older students also sat the exam – often because they had not done well in it first time round. The publishers also realised that the existing textbooks were inappropriate for these older students – both the content and presentation were usually aimed at the younger (mid-teen) market – and so they produced a textbook for English GCSE aimed at the more mature market. This is a classic example of niche publishing made possible by a detailed understanding of the market.

It is also important to know how courses are examined or assessed. In particular, it helps to know the schemas or sets of criteria used for marking students' work. Textbook authors can use these documents to determine the adequacy of their prospective books. To what extent would the book help a student to achieve (a) the lowest grade, (b) the average grade and (c) the highest grade on the courses on which the textbook is to be used? A textbook does not, of course, have to suit students of all abilities – publishers quite often market a book specifically for one segment of the ability range – but it is important to know *which* part(s) of the ability range a book suits.

It is also helpful to know the type of students likely to use the book, especially their likely educational level and background knowledge at the start of their courses. One major series of textbooks that I have commissioned for a subject at university level grew out of a report on the typical educational attainment of students enrolling in that subject. We realised that their level of intellectual confidence and their degree of literacy were often way below those required by the textbooks that were already on the market.

In addition, it is helpful to know how dependent on the textbook a student is likely to be. On some courses – perhaps when a student is following a distance-learning course or is studying for professional exams in his or her own time – the textbook might be the only resource available. At the other extreme, students might receive hundreds of hours tuition, have the opportunity to work with peers and have access to a library and the internet. Both the content and form of the ideal textbook will depend on these factors. A good example is provided by a textbook mentioned above – the one published especially for mature students of GCSE English. The book includes material relating to adult issues, such as how to apply for a job. It also includes explanations of GCSE syllabuses, how the book relates to such syllabuses and how to present coursework to the examination boards. In books for younger students, much of this explanation would be provided by a class teacher instead.

The importance of knowing the context in which a textbook will be used helps to explain further a paradox in textbook publishing that we have already touched on, namely the question of why textbooks written by subject experts are often not the best. One explanation is that experts often do not work in the context in which their books will be used by most students. Thus the textbooks they produce may be impeccable in terms of scholarship and yet, because they do not dovetail with the students' circumstances, fail to do the job that their readers require of them.

A good example of this is provided by one of my authors, who wrote a highly successful textbook about how to teach children aged 5–11. We asked him to write a similar textbook about teaching children aged 11–18. The book was markedly less successful: the author was less familiar with the courses on which the latter type of trainee teacher studied. In contrast, when one of my colleagues wanted to commission a textbook on linguistics, she deliberately chose two authors from a middle-ranking state university. When asked by a colleague why she hadn't approached someone at an Ivy-League college to write the book, she explained that more of the students expected to buy the book studied at the former type of institution. He accepted her argument: he could see that knowledge of context counts.

Knowledge, both of the subject matter and the context, is clearly of the highest importance for writing a successful textbook. It is not, however, sufficient. One also needs to be a proficient project manager.

One of the most important areas of project management skills for textbook authors is information technology (IT) skills. As we will see in subsequent chapters, these are needed for research, communication and composition. None of the essential skills is difficult to acquire. In terms of word processing, the most useful functions are probably: cutting and pasting; finding a word or phrase; word counting; checking spelling and grammar; tracking changes; and inserting a table. For using e-mail and the internet, the most useful skills are probably: searching the web for single and multiple key words; using different search engines; evaluating websites; and sending attachments.

A second important area of project management is effective management of time. The problem that causes commissioning editors to lose most sleep is slippage. It helps to know why. It is partly because of internal constraints. A commissioning editor has, for example, to:

- meet revenue targets for a given financial year – accountants can't write 'watch this space' in a company's report to share-holders
- decide which edition of a catalogue to announce a book in, when to advertise the book and when to present it to sales representatives
- sometimes publish a number of books simultaneously in order to maximise their impact on the market

It is also because of external factors – the need to publish before a competitor, for example, or in time for a book to be adopted onto reading lists at the start of the academic year. The most important aspect of time management for an author, then, is to ensure that the deadline that he or she negotiates with the publisher is realistic – a point that will be discussed more fully in Chapter 3.

A third important aspect of project management is organisation. It is no accident that perhaps my most successful textbook author is the most organised. For example, it is significant that, if he is writing to me about more than one of his books he encloses more than one letter – he only ever discusses one book per letter. This is to make filing easier. I like working with him because he never mislays anything I send him. He always has information at his fingertips with which to check his royalty statements. I don't know whether anyone has ever conducted research to see whether there is any correlation between authors' capacities to (i) write organised prose, (ii) organise material into a coherent book and (iii) organise themselves, but in my experience the correlation is strong.

Implicit in all of the aspects of the project management mentioned above is a commitment to quality on the part of authors. To succeed, a textbook needs to earn the trust of reviewers, teaching staff and students. The use that is made of a textbook is often searching, even exhaustive. Weaknesses will always be noticed. Writers in some genres can get away with substandard passages – a couple of inspired lines might redeem a mediocre song, for example – but a textbook that mixes substandard passages with flashes of brilliance is simply a substandard textbook, full stop. Your readers need to feel they can trust your product.

Case study

It is helpful at this stage to look at the type of author who attracts publishers. A good example is Sarah McNamara, who I commissioned to write a book on adolescent stress. The book, entitled *Stress in Young People*, is aimed at teachers, youth and social workers, and trainees in these professions.

Below is Sarah's description of herself, taken from her book proposal. Ask yourself which features in this description suggest that Sarah McNamara would make a successful author.

About the author
Dr Sarah McNamara BA, MA, DPhil (Oxon). Researcher at the Children's Research Centre, Trinity College Dublin, Ireland. Has been working in the area of adolescent mental health and prevention for six years (in Trinity College Dublin; the Prince's Trust (Business in the Community); University of Oxford; and for the Department of Education, Ireland). Has worked with schools, educational and clinical psychologists, guid-

ance counsellors, social workers, youth workers and psychiatrists. Awarded PhD in adolescent psychology (stress interventions) at University of Oxford (1999). Has designed, delivered and evaluated stress reduction intervention programmes for young people.

Relevant publications
- *Stress Management Programme for Secondary Schools* FalmerRoutledge (2001).

- 'The social contact patterns of young people: effects of participation in the social institutions of family, education and work'. Chapter with N. Emler in *Youth and Life Management: Research Perspectives* edited by Helena Helve and John Bynner, Helsinki University Press (1996).

- *Report into the Needs of Young People in Carlow* (in press), Children's Research Centre (1999).

- *Evaluation of the 8–15 Early School Leavers Initiative: Phase 1*, Children's Research Centre (1999).

Member of
- Society for Research on Adolescence (SRA)
- Trust for the Study of Adolescence (TSA)
- European Association of Social Psychology (EASP)

My thinking when I read this description went as follows. There is no doubt about the author's subject knowledge: she has plenty of work experience (six years) and a high level qualification (PhD), recently awarded (1999). The fact that she has completed a PhD shows that Sarah can see long projects through to completion and organise lengthy pieces of writing. She is also close to the market that the book would sell to, having worked with a variety of professionals in the field. And Sarah is well positioned to help the publisher reach that market, because she belongs to several networks. In addition, she has written for publication, including in book form. Finally, she has an international perspective, having worked in England and Ireland, been published in Finland and belonging to European networks. This suggests that the author could write a book that would sell in more than one country.

Assessing and developing yourself as a prospective textbook author

From the above discussion we can derive criteria for self-assessment. These are given below in the form of questions to ask yourself. Using the following scale:

-- = shaky
- = weak
0 = fair
+ = strong
++ = excellent

decide how you would rate:

1. your subject knowledge in terms of:
   a) depth   -- - 0 + ++
   b) breadth   -- - 0 + ++

2. your knowledge of context in terms of:
   a) syllabus(es)   -- - 0 + ++
   b) courses   -- - 0 + ++
   c) the way students are assessed   -- - 0 + ++
   d) readers' likely educational
        background/attainment   -- - 0 + ++

3. your project management skills:
   a) IT skills   -- - 0 + ++
   b) Time management   -- - 0 + ++
   c) Organisation   -- - 0 + ++

4. your commitment to quality   -- - 0 + ++

Whilst answering these questions it is useful to consider your experiences beyond writing. In the case of 3 (b), for example, you may well have worked on other long-term projects that involved firm deadlines.

If your ratings tend towards the positive end of the scale, you are probably already suited to textbook authorship. If your ratings tend towards the left-hand side of the scale, the best move is to use the advice given below to help design an action plan to develop yourself as a writer.

If you gave yourself low ratings on the questions that concern subject knowledge, there is no magic solution. There is simply no substitute for patiently increasing your familiarity through reading or working with the subject matter. If, on the other hand, you gave yourself low ratings for knowledge of context, the solution lies in research. Detailed advice on how and what to research is given in Chapter 2.

If you have identified IT skills as an area in which you need to develop, you might well find colleagues who can teach you the basic functions that you need to master. In addition, the notes at the back of this book suggest books and websites that provide guidance. If all else fails, a short introductory course at your local college or business training centre should be sufficient – and a profitable investment in time.

Time management

If it is your time management that you need to develop, then most of the useful advice can be found in general guides to time management. Examples of such guides are provided in the Notes. There are, however, certain aspects of time management that apply specifically to writers. Although there are no hard and fast rules, research suggests that productive writers tend to:

- discover good habits by seeking advice from other writers
- share drafts of their writing with colleagues
- write regularly (usually, 'little and often')

The last point is especially important. For example, most writers can easily produce 500 words of draft material in a one-hour session – especially if, instead of reading the newspaper or aimlessly drinking coffee, they have spent a few minutes thinking about what they are going to write. At that rate, if they write for three hours a week, they can write over 75 000 words a year. (As a point of comparison, this book contains about 55 000 words.)

In *Becoming a Writer*, Dorothea Brande suggests beginning by writing for a set period at the same time every day. Once you have disciplined yourself to do that, you can, she suggests, write at a different time each day, provided you always set yourself an exact time. For her, the important point is to make a promise to yourself and then stick to it. If, for example, you have decided that you will start writing at noon, don't delay until five past.

Most writers can benefit from developing simple routines for the beginning and end of each session. It is often useful to begin each session with a brief exercise. For many writers, this means beginning with a 'freewrite', i.e. a session of, say, four minutes consisting of writing without pause for correction, revision, thinking or any other kind of interruption. Personally, I prefer to begin sessions by making revisions to the text that I produced in the previous session.

It is also often useful to finish a session before you have written everything you want to write. This will make you look forward to the next session. Many writers formalise this procedure by ending a session in the middle of a paragraph or even in the middle of a sentence.

Finally

I hope that this chapter has shown that, although textbook writing can be challenging, you do not need to be superhuman to succeed. Because the emphasis has been on the challenges facing authors, it is worth underlining that the rewards of writing textbooks can be considerable. In particular, let's make explicit the rewards implied in the opening paragraph of this chapter. Textbook writing is rewarding because authors can:

1. supplement their income directly through royalty payments;
2. supplement their income indirectly, and develop their career, through enhanced promotion prospects and through further commissions to write, talk, review or advise;
3. improve their own teaching;
4. gain satisfaction through helping to train or educate their readers.

There is one further reward, namely the satisfaction – through having one's name in print and one's book on other people's shelves – of a desire for self-publicity or even immortality. This is less often admitted to than, say, the desire to contribute to the educational development of the nation, but I am certain that it is a widespread motivation for writing – and I can see nothing wrong with it. Indeed, as a commissioning editor I rather welcome it: it tells me the author is serious.

2. Research

I mentioned in Chapter 1 that, by the end of the writing process, some authors seem to carry the entire contents of their book in their heads. It would be remarkable, however, if any one 'knew it all' before they started writing. In practice, every textbook author needs to do some research. The aim of this chapter is simply to explain *what* to research and *how* to research it.

We need to be clear what we mean by 'research'. When somebody says that he or she is 'going to do some research', this could refer to one of two things:

1. finding out something that he or she doesn't know by consulting an established source of information, i.e. by drawing on what somebody else has already found out. For example, an author might 'research' how many students enrol on a particular course by calling the institution that runs it;
2. finding out something that nobody knows, i.e. conducting original research. For example, a social psychologist might conduct a survey to establish employees' perceptions of a new work practice.

Of these two types of research, the textbook author will be involved only in the first.

In fact, there are good reasons why he or she should *not* pursue the second type of research (at least as a textbook author). It is worth spelling this out in some detail because the book proposals that I receive indicate that authors sometimes confuse textbooks with an alternative genre that does require original research, namely monographs.

There are two reasons why the two genres should remain distinct. First, in order to be seen by its readers as reliable, a textbook needs to concentrate on its subject's conventional wisdom. It takes time for original research findings to become incorporated into that wisdom. Before that happens, research findings tend to go through a process of examination in which they are analysed, debated and, often, challenged. No researcher, however eminent, should assume that his or her latest set of findings will enter into the subject's conventional wisdom as a matter of course. Indeed I have seen researchers (one an expert on medieval literature and one on music) present their findings to a conference and then, after discussion, withdraw them entirely because they have come to realise that they are unreliable. That is no problem at a conference (it's what conferences are for); it would be fatal for a textbook.

Second, it takes even longer for research findings to become established in syllabuses and mark schemes. At best, therefore, inclusion of original research in a textbook is likely to prove irrelevant from the point of view of readers studying for a qualification. Examination mark schemes are often too inflexible to allow much credit to be given to students who include fresh material that the examiner had not anticipated.

It is clear, then, that textbooks are distinct from monographs: the former do not provide a backdoor route to the publication of the latter. The corollary of this is that textbooks *can* succeed without their authors ever having carried out any original research. This indeed is often the case. The company that I work for has, for example, published two very successful textbooks on working with children, written by authors with no experience of original research.

Textbook authors, then, should eschew original research and concentrate instead on personal research. The latter comprises research into:

- markets
- the context in which the prospective textbook would be used
- other publications in the field
- gaps in authors' subject knowledge

In practice, the first three types tend to overlap. At this stage, however, let us consider them one at a time.

15

(a) Research into markets

Whenever I want to commission a book, I have to present it to an Acquisitions Meeting. When I do so, the first sentence of my presentation identifies the market for the proposed book. I welcome, therefore, book proposals from authors who have themselves researched the market. Often such research not only contributes to my presentation but also assures me that the authors are themselves clear as to whom they need to write for.

The best example of this type of research that I have come across came from a psychologist who proposed a book aimed at masters students. When I told him I was uncertain about the market he sent me a copy of the business plan he had written when he set up a new internationally marketed course at his university. This included research into likely student numbers in over a dozen countries. It was this research that convinced our sales director to support the proposal so that I could commission the book. In fact, this particular book was not a textbook – but the example applies to textbooks as much as to any other form of academic or professional publishing.

In searching the potential market for a textbook, the important facts for authors to discover are:

- What courses are available
- Which institutions offer them
- (At least approximately) how many students take them

Fortunately this information is usually quite easy to discover. The most useful sources are digests (in either printed or electronic form), professional institutes or associations, exam boards and government reports. The Notes provide examples.

(b) Context

Chapter 1 provided an outline of how knowledge of the context in which textbooks would be used could help authors. We saw that the most important aspects for an author to know about were: syllabuses; courses; forms of assessment; student background; and the resources and types of support available to students.

Syllabuses are usually available from examination boards. Remember to find out whether there are any syllabus changes in the offing. This is important both because there will be a time lag between an author writing a manuscript and the book being published and because the publisher will expect a textbook to have a 'backlist' life (i.e. sell for a few years before a new edition is needed). The best sources of such information are the examination boards and the education departments of national or state governments.

In addition to the syllabuses, ask for examples of test papers and the marking schemes or assessment criteria used to award grades to students at the end of their courses. Just as the syllabuses will tell you which aspects of a subject students will be required to show knowledge of, so test papers will show in which forms students will be required to show that knowledge. You can exploit this information in two ways: you can ensure that the instructional material in your textbook (for example, end-of-chapter assignments) resembles the type of tasks students will have to perform in their tests; and you can incorporate into your text model answers for students to imitate.

Many examination boards also produce annual reports written by chief examiners. These are valuable because they often indicate which parts of the exam students struggled with. This in turn often indicates a deficiency with existing materials and hence an opportunity for writers of new textbooks.

Detail about university courses is often available on the internet (see Notes). Notice, however, that those university web pages aimed at prospective students are often not the best sources. The course descriptions there tend to be bland and generalised. More useful are the pages aimed at current students (often with assignments, lecture notes and reading lists) and the course outlines accessed through a page entitled 'faculty' or 'department'.

Another important aspect of the context is the nature of the students who are going to use your textbook. The more you understand them, the more likely it is that they will understand the textbook you write. One particularly important aspect to research is the students' likely educational background. This is because, in designing a textbook, it is important to consider the role of progression, i.e. the question of how a textbook relates to its readers' prior and future learning. Ideally a textbook should:

- not assume knowledge on the part of its readers that they do not have
- connect with the knowledge they do have
- develop their knowledge to a higher level
- prepare them for the learning they would do if they proceeded to enrol on a higher course

These points may sound obvious, but in fact textbook authors often fail to give them due attention.

An example of the value of such thinking is shown by the case of a book that I commissioned on the sociology of education. When its authors proposed it to me, they claimed that it would suit both undergraduate students and those on masters courses. I was immediately suspicious: in my experience, successful textbooks usually suit only one level of student and authors who try writing for more than one level are likely to end up satisfying nobody. However, there was enough promise in the proposal for me to suggest to the authors that we met. When I challenged the authors on this point, they put forward the following argument:

1. In the UK, there are two kinds of courses on education below masters level: (a) social scientific courses and (b) vocational courses (i.e. teacher training). The first tend to include extensive study of sociology, the second don't. Their book was aimed at the first type of course.
2. However, many of the students who enrol later on masters courses in education are teachers who previously followed the second (vocational) kind of course. Because masters courses often require an understanding of sociology, these students need a book at the start of the course to introduce them to the subject – in other words, they needed a book at undergraduate level.

This argument played an important part in my decision to commission the book. This was a classic example of the importance of the authors' understanding of context. The authors' only mistake was not to include the above argument in their initial proposal.

In *An Introduction to a Mathematical Treatment of Economics* G. C. Archibald and Richard G. Lipsey show a sound knowledge of the kinds of study that their readers will want to move onto after reading their book. In their introduction they write:

> We hope that the student who perseveres with this book will subsequently be able to...
>
> (a) take, if he wishes (and university regulations permit), a course in mathematical economics which would normally be closed to him;
>
> (b) take, if he wishes (and regulations permit), his university's first-year mathematics course during his third year...
>
> (c) read an elementary text in mathematical statistics

and so on (p.5). Such a firm grasp of readers' exit routes has clearly helped the authors to decide what to include in the book and what level to pitch it at.

To research your prospective students' likely educational backgrounds:

- Contact some of the people (enrolment officers or admissions tutors, for example) who accept students onto the courses which your textbook will support. Ask them which courses their students are likely to have studied previously.
- Read the syllabuses and then the mark schemes, assessment criteria or standards provided for those courses. Remember that (unless you are writing a niche product aimed specially at high-achieving students) most of your readers will not have achieved the top grades on these lower level courses. To understand the likely knowledge base of your average reader, concentrate on the standards specified for the middle grades of such courses.

- Study the textbooks used on those courses. Remember that your average reader will not have understood, or even have read, all of such books.

A further aspect of context that is useful to research is the nature and level of support that your readers will receive, either from resources or from tutorial staff. Books that are used primarily for independent study tend to look very different from books that are used to support courses that are heavily taught. The former need to explain everything so that it is self-evident; the latter may do little more than provide exercises for students to complete after receiving instruction on a topic in class.

Again a proposal I received for a textbook on education provides an example of the value of such knowledge. In Britain, students on teacher training courses used to spend much of their time in college. Now, they spend much more time in schools. Each student in a school is allocated a teacher to serve as mentor. This causes a problem for the mentor, who frequently lacks the training and resources required to help the student. The author, John Wilson, therefore proposed a textbook comprising: (a) a series of short readings which could be used by students and mentors as the basis for a weekly discussion, (b) questions on each reading, designed not only to check comprehension but also to stimulate discussion and (c) an introduction aimed at mentors. I commissioned the book, *Key Issues in Education and Teaching* – though I moved the introduction to the back of the book so that it would not put off students who might buy the book to read on their own.

In researching the type of tuition that your prospective readers are likely to receive, it is important to consider pedagogic trends. This will help to ensure that the textbook you write will fit neatly into the courses for which it is intended. Here it is useful to consider not only the styles of instruction that predominate today, but also those likely to grow in importance over the next few years. The best guides to the former are reports published by school inspectors, together with journal articles reporting empirical research into teaching methods (see Notes). The best guides to the latter are articles by in-service teachers (or their trainers) in professional journals, especially those published by subject associations. A word of warning, however: the latter type of article tends to be written by the more avant-garde members of the profession; teaching methods tend to change less quickly than these members either hope or predict.

One useful method of researching context is to visit some of the institutions that your prospective readers attend. Lecturers' chat, students' work, library stock – all provide insights into the context in which your textbook will be used. Authors who work as inspectors or external examiners have the great advantage of making these visits as part of their paid employment. If you work in either capacity it will certainly be worth devoting time to reflecting explicitly on what your experiences have to tell you about the context for your textbook. It is no mere co-incidence that one of the authors of the book on the sociology of education mentioned above had extensive experience as an external examiner.

(c) Researching other publications

There are several reasons why you should research other text-books in your field (or, if there are no textbooks, the closest alternatives). In particular:

- You will pick up ideas that you can employ in your own book
- You can assess the strength of the competition and decide what you need to do to beat it
- You can identify niches or topic areas neglected by other books
- You can begin to prepare your book proposal. As we will see in the next chapter, publishers will require an analysis of the competition before they decide whether to commission your book. They will ask you to evaluate competing volumes and to explain how the book you propose to write will be different and/or better
- You can see which publishers are most active in your field

There are several sources for finding out what is already available on the market. *Books in Print* is a comprehensive bibliographic source. It is also expensive, which means that by no means all libraries will stock it. It is likely, however, that your bookseller will have a copy of the CD-ROM. I strongly recommend choosing a quiet time of day to talk to him or her: explain your project and ask whether you can use the CD-ROM briefly. Most booksellers will be happy to help a local author, not least because your book might become a source of revenue for them. Do remember, however, that booksellers are there to sell books! In particular, take care to ensure that you are not in the way when there are customers around.

Booksellers themselves are also a valuable, and much over-looked, source of both information and opinion. Provided you pick the right time of day, many booksellers are very happy to have someone recognise and value their expertise. Ideally you should try to talk to the member of staff who decides which books to stock in that part of the shop in which your own book would be shelved. Ask the bookseller which textbooks sell well, how customers choose between them and what comments they've heard about particular books. Above all, ask the $64 000 question: is there any feature or quality that customers say they are looking for in a textbook but cannot find?

Internet bookstores are also helpful sources of information. Their sites are particularly useful for finding out about books published abroad. Both the quality and range of material does, however, vary. On amazon.com, for example, it is best not to trust the reviews, many of which are posted by authors, their friends (and enemies) and their publishers. Do remember that amazon.com is not the only site (some others are listed in the Notes), although the fact that it gives a sales rank for each book is helpful: it will help you to assess the strength of the competition, provided you do not use it to make fine judgements between books (the sales rank, after all, reflects sales over one period of time through one retailer using one medium).

Publishers' websites are also useful sources of information (see Notes). Many authors ignore these on the assumption that, because they are commercial, they will be biased. Of course, each publisher will promote its product in the best possible light. Even this is useful to find out about, since it will tell you what the publisher believes to be the strength of the book against which yours will have to compete. Many sites contain more information than that. For example, some include e-mails posted by lecturers, teachers and students. This will help you to understand the way the market responds to, and uses, text-books in your field.

Information *about* books in print is very useful, but it is no substitute for studying the books themselves. Once you have received a contract from a publisher (see the next chapter), it will be useful to buy copies of the best of the competing volumes. Before contract, however, you may be reluctant to spend a lot of money buying these books. Remember that most libraries, even if they don't stock the books you want, can obtain books for you through inter-library loans service. Alternatively, it is often possible to locate second-hand copies (see Notes for website addresses) – though do make sure you obtain the most recent edition. Library and, especially, second-hand copies have the advantage that they have often been marked or written on by previous readers. Their markings provide clues as to what those readers think about the books.

Once you have acquired a copy of a competing book, how should you study it? First, note the basic facts, starting with the title, subtitle, publisher and price. Look at the imprint page to discover the date of the current edition. Check also where it has been published, how many editions it has been through, how many times it has been reprinted and whether the book is available in hardback, softback or both. Then note the number of pages and the number and type of illustrations of all types (charts, graphs, flow diagrams, photographs, drawings and so on). After that, note which topics the book covers. The best way to do this is to develop a grid. On the left-hand side, list every topic that could be covered by the book (this list will be derived from your knowledge of courses on which this book might be used) with one row for each topic. Across the top, list each competing book, allowing one column per book. In each square, record whether the book covers that topic or not. Use a star system ranging from one star (meaning the book mentions a topic) to three stars (meaning there is extensive discussion of a topic).

With the strongest books, it is worth comparing the latest edition to an early edition. Consider how it has changed. Developments between editions often provide clues about trends in the field. Note that textbook editions often follow a cycle. Textbooks often improve over the first couple of editions as the author responds to feedback from reviewers and colleagues. After several editions, however, a book can start to look dated: the author might try to respond to changes in the subject by tinkering with the contents within the original structure, whereas in fact a more wholesale change might be necessary. The big prizes in textbook publishing go to people who spot that a standard work is beginning to look dated and that a new model is needed.

After you have noted the facts, move on to consider your opinions. Start with the positive aspects. What impresses you about the book? Concentrate your thoughts on those aspects of textbooks that we listed at the beginning of the book as the most fundamental. Ask yourself:

1. How authoritative is it?
2. How comprehensive?
3. How well pitched is it?
4. How clear is it?
5. How organised?
6. How up to date?

Then consider what else strikes you about the book.

Next, consider the book's shortcomings. Focus your thoughts on the same set of questions. Next, consider what could have been different. What could the author have added, or omitted, or altered? Finally, consider the book as a whole. Skim through your notes, glance again at the contents page, flick through the pages, close the book and ask yourself: how would you describe this book in a nutshell?

Fig. 2.1 summarises the main points to consider about each book that you evaluate.

As well as the books themselves, pay attention to the reviews that they received, especially in professional newsletters and journals. These reviews will show both what textbook users

Title: Author(s):	Today's date: / /2

Information
* Subtitle
* Publisher
* Format: hardback/softback
* Date of edition
* No. of editions
* No. of impressions of
  current edition
* Where published
* No. of (a) pages and
  (b) illustrations
* Price(s)
* Other
	What could have been...
	
	* Added?
	
	* Omitted?

Strengths * Authoritative? * Comprehensive? * Well pitched? * Clarity? * Organisation? * Up to date? * Other	* Altered?
Weaknesses * Unauthoritative? * Not comprehensive? * Poorly pitched? * Obscurity? * Disorganised? * Dated? * Other	**Overall** Summarise this book in a few words

Fig. 2.1: Pro forma for evaluating textbooks

value in textbooks and what weaknesses existing books have. You want to make sure that you satisfy the former and capitalise on the latter.

Reviews provide formal, and usually fairly expert, feedback. It is also useful to look for informal feedback. Talk to teachers or lecturers who use the books on their courses and the students who actually study from them. I once commissioned a textbook on teaching English as a second language because an international agency reported that teachers it employed on three different continents had all indicated the lack of a suitable textbook for their particular level of teaching.

Researching gaps in your subject knowledge

An author who is seriously considering writing a textbook is likely to be educated to a reasonably high level already. It is likely, therefore, that you already know how to find out more about your subject. Since, however, most people's learning through inquiry has, until recently, been dominated by the use of printed matter (books, articles and dissertations), it is worth considering two other types of source, namely experts in person and websites.

The advantage of consulting experts is that, in addition to explaining some aspect of your subject, they might well have views on how the field is developing in general. The disadvantage is that their concern to keep up with change in their subject sometimes leads them to overestimate recent developments.

An advantage of websites is that they are often updated regularly. The main disadvantage is that it is difficult to assess their reliability. That is true of books too, but if a book is published by a press with a scholarly reputation – Oxford University Press, for example – you know at least that the book will have been selected carefully and reviewed and edited by professionals. Such a press can ill-afford to damage its brand name by publishing shoddy books. Websites, in contrast, are often one-off affairs and it is not always easy to discover even who they are published by. Fortunately there exist some websites designed to help assess the reliability and quality of other websites (see the Notes).

Case study

Finally, by way of example, I will outline the research that went into a series of textbooks that I published dealing with the study of children's literature. Three main types of research went into this series. The series editor and I researched:

- Booksellers' views
- Existing books
- The courses on which the books would be used

Visits to booksellers revealed uncertainty on their part as to where to shelve books on children's literature. Sometimes they were shelved under literary studies, sometimes under education and sometimes with parenting and childcare books. We realised that it was essential throughout the project to make the market for the series (in fact, students of literature) clear.

Our research into existing books was facilitated by a list in Peter Hunt, *Introduction to Children's Literature* of the most influential studies of children's literature. Given this list, we were able to choose a cross-section and consider what typified such books. We supplemented this research by using bibliographies and publishers' catalogues to gain an overall view of books in print in this area. This enabled us to identify a gap in the market. On the one hand, there were plenty of introductions to, and historical surveys of, the field in general; on the other hand, there were some specialist monographs about individual authors or particular periods. In the middle, however, there was a lack of textbooks for undergraduate students for whom the first type of books were too general and the second type were too specialised. As a result, we commissioned a series of textbooks covering genres (e.g. horror, fantasy) designed to form a bridge between the two types of books already available.

In order to ensure that the books we had in mind would be suitable, we visited some of the colleges that taught children's literature and also visited websites of foreign universities offering similar courses. This convinced us that our decision to concentrate on genre studies was accurate: lecturers and students often did approach children's literature in this way and yet their reading lists revealed a lack of suitable textbooks.

In the above case study, the research was split between the publisher (me, as commissioning editor) and the series editor. However, all of this type of research could be conducted by authors – and the more such research authors do, the more likely are publishers to accept their proposals. In fact, what happened in this case was that my research corroborated what the series editor had told me, with the result that I developed a strong trust in her series proposal.

3. Approaching and Working with Publishers

You might be surprised that I have placed this chapter before those on the actual writing of your textbook. Surely, you might ask, you can't approach a publisher about a book that hasn't yet been written?

Although this is a very natural assumption, the truth is the other way round: you would be unwise to write a book until you have approached a publisher. This is so fundamental that it is worth understanding the reasoning behind it.

The main reason why you should not write your book first (or, at least, not write very much of it – we will look at the case for sample chapters below) is that you risk wasting a lot of time. However confident you may be that a publisher will want to publish your book, you have no guarantee that they will until you have been offered a contract. It is entirely possible to devote hundreds of hours to writing a manuscript only to find that there are no takers for it. People sometimes say – or at least tell themselves – that they don't mind this and that the pleasure lies simply in the writing. I suppose this might be true of expressive writing such as novels and memoirs – but it is difficult to believe that anyone would write a textbook just for fun.

A second reason for approaching publishers before you write a book is a variation of the first. It may be that a publisher accepts your idea for a book but insists on some changes. For example, the editor might require you to take out some chapters or to change the emphasis or the structure of at least part of the book. In each case, you will have wasted time if you have already written a complete manuscript.

There is one exception to the rule of approaching publishers before writing. That is when a lecturer or teacher is proposing a book that is based on resources he or she has written for another purpose – lecture notes, for example, or learning resources for students on courses they teach. Even here the conversion of such texts into a manuscript for a book is likely to require plenty of work. If so, the same rule applies: approach a publisher before doing the extra work.

One further reason for not writing your manuscript beforehand is that a publisher who is offered a complete manuscript can see that the author has done the bulk of his or her work. This puts you in a weak position when it comes to negotiating royalties. You can hardly argue that you need a hefty advance to cover research costs, for example, when it is clear that you've already done the research. An author who can no longer say 'If that's all you're going to offer, it's not worth my while writing the book' has lost one of his or her most powerful negotiating cards.

All of the above reasons explain why authors who are well informed about publishing do not approach publishers with their manuscripts complete. And this very fact provides a further reason for you doing likewise: that is, if you do write your manuscript first, you risk appearing naïve in the eyes of publishers.

It is best, therefore, to approach a publisher before writing your manuscript. To do this you will require a book proposal. Before you write even that, however, you should decide which publishers you are going to approach. The reason for making that decision first is that textbook types vary so much between publishing houses. If you have researched the books in print as described in the previous chapter, you will have noticed that the typical length, style, format and presentation of books vary between publishers. The differences between publishing houses are especially clear when, as is often the case, textbooks are published as a part of a series. Books within a series are likely to be standardised, not only in terms of cover and text design, but also in terms of contents and structure. There is likely to be a series policy on the type of illustrations used, for example.

Because of these differences it is advisable to tailor the proposal you write to the preferences of the particular publisher you are writing to. If, for example, a publisher has a series of textbooks, each of which contains twenty or so short chapters, it is unwise to send a proposal for a book consisting of six long chapters. It is for this reason that I suggest you decide which publishers you are going to approach before you write your proposal.

How to select a publisher

The first task is to discover which publishers are active in the field in which you wish to publish. The research outlined in the previous chapter will have revealed many of the relevant publishers. To develop a complete list it is necessary to do some further research. Several printed and on-line reference sources will help you to do this (see Notes). The most useful are those that enable you to search lists of publishers by category.

Once you have generated a list of publishers for your book, the question is how to choose between them. Ask yourself which publishers are most active in the kinds of market you envisage for your book. Ideally, you will find a publisher that has several books that are comparable to yours but nothing quite the same. Consider the following examples:

- You wish to write a history textbook aimed at a certain school grade. You discover a publisher with textbooks aimed at the same grade in analogous subjects – geography or social studies, for example – but not in history.
- You wish to write a professional textbook on counselling aimed at an intermediate level. You discover a publisher with counselling textbooks at an introductory and advanced level, but not an intermediate one.
- You wish to write a university-level textbook on a certain area of economics – say, international trade. You discover a publisher with textbooks covering other areas of the subject (finance, for example) at the same level, but not in your area.

In each situation, you have discovered the ideal publisher to approach.

Often the situation is more awkward. It may be, for example, that the publisher already has a textbook on the same subject and at the same level as your book. It might well be that such a publisher would not wish to publish your book as well. Why would any publisher go to the expense of producing a book that will compete against one of its own books? However, you need not assume that this is the case. It may be that the existing book is going out of date or simply is not very good. I have commissioned a textbook in a subject in which we already had one book in print (with hundreds of copies in the warehouse) because I did not think the first book was good enough. By commissioning a new book I was in effect deciding that we would have to pulp most of the copies of the existing book, but I would rather do that than keep losing sales to our competitors.

It may also be that, on closer inspection (of the type outlined in the first chapter), certain key differences emerge between your book and the one already published – in which case the books might complement, rather than compete against, each other. At least the existence of the first book is evidence that the publisher is active in your area. That said, if the choice is between a publisher with a particular gap in its list and one that has already published a potential competitor to your book, there is no question which to approach first.

Consider too the reputation and image of the publisher. Start with your own reactions. What do you think about the books that publisher has produced? Do you find them usable? Do you like their design? Do they use strong authors? I chose A & C Black as the first publisher to approach with the proposal for this book because they commission top-notch authors – the book on crime fiction in this series, for example, is written by a big-name novelist (H.R.F. Keating) – and I noted too that, as publishers of long-established and highly reputable reference books such as *Who's Who?*, they had a reputation for quality.

If you work in an institution (or visit conferences) where you meet publishers' sales representatives, ask yourself what these meetings tell you. If one rep is well-informed, enthusiastic and much in evidence, whereas another seems not to have been briefed, fails to exude confidence in his or her products, and is rarely seen, that is a pretty good reason for preferring the first publishing house to the second. Similarly, it is worth reflecting on your experience of publishers' policies on inspection copies.

For a textbook to succeed, it needs to get onto course reading lists. This will only happen if teachers, lecturers or tutors have had a good look at the book. To do this, they need inspection copies. A publisher that does not have a clearly explained and smoothly running inspection copy policy will not succeed in selling many textbooks.

It is also useful to consult colleagues, readers and people in the book trade. Ask colleagues which textbooks they like using and whether they have ever worked (as a reviewer or consultant, for example) for any of the publishers you are considering. If so, what has been their experience? Ask students which books they like using, which ones they found easy to get hold of and which ones they consider good value. Ask booksellers which publishers they like stocking and which reps they are happy to see. If a publisher has an inefficient warehouse and distribution system, for example, or overprices its books or gives them lousy covers, booksellers will be less keen to stock their books.

Unless you work in a very specialist area, you will find that your initial research using digests of publishers will produce quite a long list of potential outlets for your book. Equally, unless you work in a very popular area, you will find that your subsequent research, as outlined above, will reduce this to a shortlist. The question then arises whether you should approach more than one of the publishers on your shortlist at the same time.

Opinions differ on this. There are two good reasons for approaching more than one publisher at a time. The first concerns time: if your proposed book is time-sensitive (it has to be ready for the start of a new course, for example), you might well not want to wait for any one publisher to make a decision before approaching the next. The second reason is the obvious one: if your proposal elicits serious interest from more than one publisher simultaneously you are effectively in a position to auction your book to the highest bidder.

On the other hand, there are strong reasons for not approaching publishers simultaneously. If you tell the editor that you have approached another company, he or she might be reluctant to invest time in considering the proposal, sending it to reviewers and so on, only to find that another publisher has signed up the book. Equally, if you do not tell the editor what you are up to and it subsequently emerges, the mistrust that this creates can damage your chances of publication.

The strongest reason for approaching only one publisher at a time is that it gives you a chance to strengthen your proposal every time you receive feedback. Anything other than a blunt rejection letter is likely to provide valuable feedback. A publisher might provide reasons for not commissioning your project, in which case you can consider whether you wish to revise your proposal before sending it elsewhere. A rejection letter might also include suggestions of where else to send the proposal (although such suggestions are often rather perfunctory). Most valuable of all, a publisher might include detailed reviewers' evaluations of your proposal.

On balance, it is best, unless a book is particularly time-sensitive, to approach only one publisher at a time.

How to approach a publisher

Once you have decided which publisher(s) to approach, there are three ways of proceeding: you can make an inquiry, send a proposal or send a proposal with sample chapters. Often the decision over which method to use is made for you by the publisher. Many publishers state on their websites or in their entries in reference books such as the *Writers' & Artists' Yearbook* which methods they prefer or which methods they dislike. If a publisher has stated a preference, respect it.

An inquiry letter outlines the proposed book in order to see whether an editor would like to receive a full proposal for a certain book. The outline is necessarily brief: the whole point of an inquiry letter is to save the editor from having to read the whole proposal at the outset. The outline will describe the subject matter of the proposed book and identify its intended market. Good inquiry letters are concise and no more than one page in length.

The advantage of sending an inquiry letter is that (provided editors actually reply) it quickly identifies those publishers who would definitely not be interested in the book. This enables you to focus on the publishers most likely to commission the book. However, I do question the value of inquiry letters. As an editor I find that, precisely because they lack detail, they allow me to eliminate only the most obviously inappropriate proposals – and any author who has done the research recommended above should be able to do that for him or herself. I dislike inquiries because they double my correspondence: I have to reply first to the inquiry and then to the subsequent proposal. Why not just send the proposal in the first place?

The second method of approach is the book proposal. Some publishers welcome free-form proposals, others insist that authors use a standardised form. The latter is usually obtainable from the publisher's website. Whichever form a proposal takes, the information required remains the same. In order to consider a book for publication, a publisher needs to know:

- The working title
- Content: what the book will be about
- Market: who is going to buy it
- Competition: how it will compare with other books
- The author: who will write it
- The time-scale: when the manuscript will be ready
- Production requirements: how long the manuscript will be and how many illustrations will be required and of what sort

Let's look in detail at what is implied by each of these requirements.

Working title

I specify 'working' title because publishers often have their own ideas on titles. In particular, books within a series have standardised titles. Most successful textbooks have very short titles that make it clear what the book is about and, perhaps, what level the book is pitched at. If you are writing on, say, economics at an introductory level, it is best to make the working title simply 'Introductory Economics'. There might, of course, already be books with that title, but that is not necessarily a problem.

Many textbooks also have subtitles. If you give yours a subtitle, ensure that it does not narrow the appeal of your book. For example, there is a very successful textbook by Michael Haralambos entitled *Sociology*. Its subtitle – *themes and perspectives* – confirms the sense given by the main title that the book will be wide-ranging. In contrast, a book entitled *Sociology: a Weberian approach* would sound much narrower.

The advantage of a subtitle is that it helps to differentiate your book from its competitors and it can provide a few extra key words that would enable customers to locate your book in an electronic search. Since, however, some bibliographical software carries only main titles, do ensure that the most important one or two key words for your book figure in your main title.

Content

In my experience, authors very rarely fail to include in their proposals enough about the content of the proposed book. If anything, the problem tends to be the other way round: some authors include too much about the content, to the exclusion of almost everything else. To outline the content it is usually sufficient to include a brief synopsis of the book as a whole, followed by the proposed contents page, plus a few sentences characterising each chapter. Often the best way to outline a chapter is simply by giving the subheadings that will feature in the chapter. Points of detail are best left until later in the negotiation process.

Market

When describing the proposed readership for the book, be precise. Sometimes, in seeking to convince the publisher that there is a sufficient market for a book, authors blur distinctions. For example, they might claim that a book will be suitable both for senior grades in high school and for freshmen at college. In practice, it is very rare for a textbook to work with both groups. If you find yourself claiming that your book would work for a dual market, pause and ask yourself whether it is really possible to write such a text. Often the simple exercise of writing a few sample pages will reveal that the challenge of satisfying disparate audiences requires an impossible juggling act.

Consider, for example, *Creating Texts* by Walter Nash and David Stacey. The publisher's blurb presents the book as suitable not only for students in higher education but also for those in their final years of high school. Chapter 1 begins:

> Let us suppose that you are about to write, at the request of your insurance company (Brightside Brokers), a brief factual description of what happened when your motor vehicle was rear-ended... You are of course wholly innocent of any responsibility for this deplorable event, which occurred while you were singing along to some old Leonard Cohen tapes... All you know is that a big car came up behind you and removed your rear bumper, your stop lights, and most of your baggage compartment, including...those pretty flowering baskets you were carrying home from the garden centre.

Leonard Cohen? Flowering baskets? Is this *really* going to be a book to suit high school students as well as those at college?

This is not to say that textbooks only ever have a single market. It *is* to say that the needs of the readers comprising each market need to be broadly similar. It is also to say that you need to be clear about the distinctions between each group of readers. If you feel that there is more than one market for your book, distinguish between the main markets and the subsidiary ones. For an editor to offer you a contract, he or she will need to take your proposal to an acquisitions meeting and state there what the main market for the book is. If your proposal provides a clear, bold, sentence that the editor can lift out to use at the meeting, you are giving your proposal a real chance of success. Such a sentence will not only help to gain a contract, but also help to ensure that the publisher makes a success of the book. The most successful textbooks are those on which all elements of the publishing house – especially the editorial, design, marketing and sales departments – are clear and in agreement about the market for the book they are publishing.

Authors rarely include quantitative information about markets in their proposals. This is an oversight. No book will ever get commissioned without the support of the publisher's sales director. Sales directors tend to think in terms of numbers. Your proposal will make more impact if you can support it quantitatively. How many institutions offer courses for which your book could be used? How many students study these courses each year?

Throughout the section on markets, you should include information about the potential your book has for sales in foreign markets. Publishers makes sales abroad either by exporting directly or through co-publication, i.e. by selling the rights to your title in certain territories so that another publisher can publish there. Either way, these sales are important to publishers for two reasons: they not only provide revenue, but also, by extending the print run, reduce the unit costs of producing your book and so make those copies sold at home more profitable too. In addition to this, publishers like to earn subsidiary income by selling translation rights.

Authors based in England need to remember that other parts of the UK have their own education systems. For an author based in the US, the first challenge is to ensure that the proposed book works in more than one state (so that, for example, a book written by an author familiar with the education system in Texas sells also in California). The second challenge is to recognise that there is a sizeable and often overlooked export market on the doorstep, namely Canada.

The problem is that textbooks often do not export well, for the simple reason that education and examination systems vary between countries. Generally speaking, the higher up the education system the book is designed to be used at, the more likely it is to export. The export potential of textbooks for masters courses is much greater than those aimed at high school examination classes. In any case, it is worth thinking what you can do to maximise the export potential of your book and then highlighting this in your proposal. For example, there are a number of international schools around the world that use British-based examinations boards. If you know that a large number of overseas students are entered for the syllabuses your book is designed to cover, that is certainly worth alerting the publisher to.

As one researches different national standards, curricula and assessment systems, it is easy to become depressed: the differences can make one doubt that any book will be able to sell into more than one market. In fact, however, virtually any book will sell at least some copies abroad. For example, my company published a textbook on childcare aimed entirely at the UK market and based on national standards in the UK. It turned out, however, that the book was also suitable for trainee care workers in Georgia, USA. How much better it would have been if all concerned had known that from the start!

An awareness of differences should not blind one to the common elements between countries. Whatever the variations between mathematics curricula, for example, it remains true that students in all countries are required to learn to add, subtract, multiply and divide.

Competition

In providing an analysis of competing books on the market, the prudent course of action is to be candid. Unfortunately, not all authors are. Often there is a tendency to downplay the opposition in the belief that this will make the proposed book more attractive. This is a mistake: it makes the author appear naïve.

It is important, therefore, to provide a thorough and authoritative analysis of competing books. Throughout this analysis you should emphasise what makes your book distinctive or better. Be precise: simply saying that a book is not very good will convince nobody, whereas saying precisely what that book's deficiency is – perhaps supported with a quotation from a review, colleague or students – is very helpful. Note that it is not necessary for your book to be better than other books in every respect (and so there is no point in pretending that there is nothing good about the books already in print). What is important is that your book has at least one (and often it need only be one) important distinctive feature. It is this that will provide the Unique Selling Point (USP) that will guide the publisher's work throughout. It is vital that the USP emerges very clearly from your analysis at this stage.

Author

Tell the publisher plenty about yourself. To an important extent, a publisher offering a contract for a book is acquiring not just a manuscript but also an author. Include any information that is likely to strengthen your case, especially details of your previous publications, work experience (especially teaching, training and examining), qualifications and the networks you belong to. The last item in this list is important because it will suggest ways in which you can help to market and promote the book after it is written.

A word here should be said about which types of previous publications you should mention. Often the career of textbook authors follows a continuum along the following lines. First come what may be called humble beginnings: writing worksheets for one's own students and sharing them with colleagues or perhaps posting them on a web page. After that tends to come small-scale projects: using materials for an in-service training session or conference workshop; writing articles or book reviews in newsletters, professional magazines or journals; and perhaps acting as a consultant for a publisher. Beyond that comes involvement in books as contributor, editor or author. The further down this continuum you have developed, the stronger your credentials for having your book proposal published. Wherever you have reached on this continuum, it is important to provide the publisher with details of that work. If you have not published anything before, you must include information about activities analogous to publication. Often, for example, school textbooks have their origins in the learning materials that the teacher produces for his or her classroom. Similarly college textbooks sometimes have their origin in a lecturer's course notes.

It may be that you are considering co-authoring your book. There is much to be said for the idea. Co-authors tend to gee each other up and help each other to stay on schedule. They also tend to exert quality control on each other's work. And, when the book is published, the publisher has two people out there with a vested interest in pushing the book. However, co-authoring does exert tensions on a relationship and so it is important for there to be a strong degree of trust and understanding between authors before the writing process begins. Actually, the process of writing the book proposal itself is likely to reveal whether the writers see the project in the same light. For this reason, it is a good idea not to leave the writing of the proposal to just one of the co-authors.

Conversely, if there are more than two authors, co-authoring is likely be prove counterproductive. Each decision tends to get referred to what is in effect a committee and delays and fudges inevitably result. As we will see in Chapter 5, it is important when writing a textbook to have a clear sense of the overall design and purpose of the text. This too becomes harder when three or more authors are involved.

Time-scale

When specifying a date for completion of the manuscript the most important point is, as I explained in Chapter 1, to be realistic. Authors tend to be over-optimistic. Often they fail to allow for the time taken by tasks other than writing the main text of the manuscript – tasks such as checking references and redrafting parts of the text, for example. They also tend to fail to allow time for contingencies – illness, for example, or problems with a computer. The best way to calculate the time needed for writing the book is to work out what seems most realistic and then add at least one third as much time again. When specifying a time-scale in your proposal, it is best to specify the amount of time it would take to write the book from receipt of the publisher's contract rather than committing to a date on the calendar. You don't know, after all, how long it will take the publisher to get round to providing a contract – and phrasing the time-scale in that way does provide the publisher with some incentive to get a move on in considering your proposal.

Production requirements

The reason for specifying the length of the manuscript and the number and type of illustrations is that the publisher needs this information to calculate the cost of producing the book – and without a costing, he or she cannot reach a rational decision over whether to publish the book. Bear in mind that the inclusion of photographs can increase production costs significantly.

Some kinds of textbooks, however, do require photographs: geography books are a good example. The rule of thumb should be that if photographs are needed to do a job of work – to illustrate something that would be difficult to show merely through words or diagrams, for example – then they are worth proposing; if, on the other hand, their main function is decorative, they are best taken out.

The above discussion outlines the principles of proposal writing. The guiding principle throughout should be to try to empathise with publishers sufficiently to anticipate what information they need and then to provide that information clearly and concisely.

It is helpful at this stage to look at an example of a book proposal. I suggest that you read the proposal in the Appendix twice, asking yourself the first time what an acquisitions editor would think of it and then considering what you as an author can learn from it.

The final issue concerning book proposals is the question of sample chapters. It is very common with textbooks for the publisher to ask to see sample chapters before commissioning the book. Some publishers' proposal notes request sample chapters as a matter of course. This serves several purposes:

- It enables the publisher to see how well the author can write. For this reason, the less that the author has published before, the more likely the publisher is to ask to see sample chapters.
- The chapters illustrate more fully what kind of book the author has in mind. In particular, it helps the publisher (and readers that the publisher is likely to send the chapters to) to gauge the tone and pitch of the proposed book.
- The chapters serve as a basis for negotiation: the publisher can discuss with the author the strengths and weaknesses of the writing and suggest revisions.
- The publisher can begin straightaway to design mock-up pages that are necessary for an accurate costing.

If you are asked to write and send sample chapters, select the first chapter and one other. The first chapter sets the key for the rest of the book. Obviously, you need at this stage to approach composition, word processing, presentation and proof-reading more scrupulously than ever.

An alternative method

Until now we have been working on the assumption that you have in mind a particular book that you wish to write. This chapter has shown how to go about getting it published. Often, however, commissioning works the other way round: the publishers decide what books they would like to commission and then go in search of authors to write them. This is particularly common in schools' publishing. The question then becomes, how do you go about ensuring that it is you that they approach?

There are various ways of becoming known to publishers. One is by being active in your profession by joining associations, attending meetings, writing articles and book reviews in journals and newsletters, and giving conference papers. A second is by approaching publishers directly by talking to reps and writing to editors. Potential authors often write letters of inquiry, not about particular books, but about the possibility of work in a certain field. Such a letter should specify:

- what subject you are interested in
- at what level you work
- what your areas of special interest are

You should certainly include a curriculum vitae specifying your academic and professional qualifications, your teaching experience and your publishing experience if you have any. You may also include examples of your own teaching resources. Since textbook publishing is increasingly becoming a multimedia business, direct the publisher to any resources you have published on the internet and to your personal website if you have one.

Another way of becoming known to a publisher is precisely the method already described above, i.e. by sending a book proposal. It is not uncommon for a publisher to reject a particular proposal but to invite the author to consider another project that the publisher has in mind.

The contract and after

Let us assume that your book proposal has been successful. You have been offered a contract. What then? This is not the place for a detailed discussion of the niceties of contracts, but it is useful to observe a few general principles.

First, do what most authors fail to do – that is, actually read your contract. Look particularly at the details concerning manuscript length, date of submission, rights, royalties and advances. Query any points that you are unsure of.

Second, remember that you are entirely free to negotiate before signing. You might, for example, suggest that your royalty rate should rise after the publisher has sold a certain number of copies – after all, if the book sells well the publisher can probably afford to pay extra. It is hardly likely that a publisher would ever withdraw the offer of a contract simply because you are seeking to negotiate terms. The act of showing that you are careful and astute will, if anything, win you respect.

You will certainly want to look closely at the royalty rate. This may be expressed as a percentage of list price (LP). For example, if a book is priced at £15, an author on 10% LP will receive £1.50. Alternatively, the royalty may be expressed as a percentage of the publisher's net receipts (NR), i.e. the amount publishers receive from retailers or wholesalers. If, for example, a book sells for £15, the retailer retains £5, and the publisher receives £10, an author on 10% NR will receive £1.

Advances against royalties may be paid on signature of the contract, on the publisher's acceptance of your manuscript or on publication. If writing the book is going to entail research costs, ask for an advance payable on signature of contract.

Royalties are not the only points open for negotiation. How many free copies of the book will you receive? How many copies of the manuscript will you have to deliver? Are you obliged to offer your next book to the same publisher? If you die, will your estate inherit all of your rights? These are points on which your editor can often afford to give ground.

Once the contract has been signed, what then? Although we tend to think of writing as a solitary process, there is in fact a good deal of teamwork involved in writing a textbook. Just consider what is implied by the term 'editor'. Most textbook writers discover that this is a very elastic, even promiscuous, title. First, the book itself might be an edited one to which several different people contribute a chapter or more. In this case, you will have – or be – a book editor. Then there is the person who commissions the book – the acquisitions editor. The book might well be part of a series, in which case there will be a series editor (usually an academic). Then there is the person who actually edits your manuscript by reading it, making corrections, raising queries and so on. This is the copy-editor. The copy-editor might well be a freelance, in which case there will be someone in the publishing house responsible for outsourcing the work and liaising with the copy-editor. This person will be the project, desk or house editor. Sometimes the same person performs more than one of these functions, but with the larger publishers it is quite possible for you to find yourself working with up to five different people, each of whom is called an editor of some description. In addition to that, you will need to liaise with other members of the publishing staff, especially the promotion and marketing department (as we will see in Chapter 11). By the time your book is published you will be very aware that authorship is a less individualistic activity than is commonly assumed.

Part Two: Composition and Design

4. Your Readers' Needs

No one reads textbooks for fun. Textbooks are read by people who need to learn – usually in order to gain some form of qualification. Authors are more likely to satisfy these people if they understand something about how they learn. The difficulty here is that most textbooks will be read by thousands of people, most of whom are unknown to the author and each of whom has his or her own style of learning. How on earth can an author planning a textbook even begin to take into account these learning styles?

Fortunately, people's learning styles fall into patterns. Knowing these patterns will help you to write books to suit all readers. One can describe these learning styles in various ways. The method outlined in this chapter is that developed by a psychologist, David Kolb. I have chosen his taxonomy of learning styles because it yields very practical conclusions for textbook authors.

Kolb provides two ways of categorising styles of learning. The first concerns the ways in which learners prefer to encounter the material they are going to learn. On the one hand, there are people who like to learn through concrete examples that show the 'nitty-gritty' of what is to be learnt. On the other hand, there are people who like to learn abstractly or theoretically. They like to learn from explanations of how concepts relate to one another. In between these two extremes, there are those who prefer to learn through a blend of concrete and abstract experience. We can therefore think of a spectrum on which we can distinguish learners' preferred modes of encountering material to be learnt:

concrete experience ◄───────► abstract conceptualisation

47

The other way of categorising learning styles is by considering what learners like to *do* with whatever it is that they are learning. Some learners like a hands-on approach in which they can be active, 'get stuck in' and try things out. Other learners prefer to stand back, observe and reflect. Again we can think of a spectrum:

active experimentation ←——→ reflective observation

We can put these two spectrums together in a diagram like this:

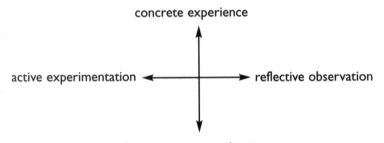

concrete experience

active experimentation ←——————→ reflective observation

abstract conceptualisation

Fig. 4.1: Types of learning

We can now use this diagram to distinguish various styles of learning. For example, a reader who preferred to learn from concrete experience rather than to learn abstractly, and who preferred to reflect on that experience rather than use it as the basis for activity, would be located in the top right-hand corner of the diagram.

This way of thinking about learning styles has two implications for the design of textbooks. The first is you should aim to include in your book a range of materials aimed at providing all four kinds of learning. To provide the opportunity to learn through concrete experience, you should include some case studies and real-life examples. To provide the opportunity to learn through abstract conceptualisation, you should provide passages of discursive prose characterised by argument, explanation and theory. To provide an opportunity to learn through reflective observation, you should create spaces that encourage readers to reflect, either on what they have just read or on what their personal experience reveals about the subject at hand. And to provide an opportunity to learn through active experimentation, you should include exercises that require the reader to *do* something (e.g. practical problem-solving or making an artefact).

Consider, for example, someone writing a chapter on supply and demand in an economics textbook. To encourage learning from concrete experience, he or she might include a case study of how property prices in an area went up when a new motorway made the area easy to commute from. This could include an interview with an estate agent or a long-time resident and perhaps also a table of statistics showing the price of certain types of property over the years. To encourage learning through abstract conceptualisation, our author could include a formal explanation of the derivation of demand and supply curves and a logical explanation of how their interaction affects the price of a commodity. To encourage learning through reflection, the writer might ask readers either to try to identify patterns in the data provided or to reflect on their own experiences of changes in price (how, for example, the price of tickets to watch the local football team went up when they were promoted to a higher league). To encourage learning through active experimentation, he or she might suggest that readers collect price data for themselves (say, through talking to traders), play Monopoly-style games, or simulate an auction.

There is nothing very new in these suggestions. Case studies, pauses for reflection, discursive prose and exercises are the staple ingredients of textbooks. Yet often I find that textbook authors need to be reminded of this. Otherwise what happens is that, until they are reminded, authors include plenty of material of the type that they themselves prefer to learn from, at the expense of the other types of material. I also find that as soon as this is pointed out to them, most textbook authors see at once the value of a balance of material and that the provision of such material is not very difficult to achieve. In fact, the challenge of providing all four types of material often turns out to be very liberating, or even therapeutic, for the author.

The second implication of Kolb's learning model is both more complicated and more controversial. It is the suggestion that, in order to maximise learning, you should not simply provide opportunities for all four types of learning, but also provide them in a certain sequence. This sequence, known as the Kolb learning cycle, is illustrated in Fig. 4.2.

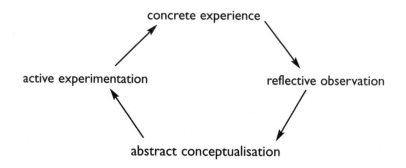

Fig. 4.2: Learning cycle

In this sequence, concrete experience provides the material to be reflected on; the reflection leads through a process of concept and pattern formation to abstract conceptualisation; the abstract theorisation produces hypotheses that can be tested through active experimentation; and the active experimentation provides new concrete experience that can again be reflected on. The idea is that, with each cycle, learning becomes more refined and advanced. Logically this provides authors with a sequence to follow. A chapter, for example, which begins the cycle at the 'concrete experience' stage with, say, a case study should follow with a pause for reflection, after which should come the discursive prose and then the suggested exercises. It may be, however, that even if you accept the logic of this cycle, you find it imposes too great a constraint on your writing. My own feeling is that it is more important to aim to include all four types of material in any one chapter than it is to provide those types of material in a particular sequence.

Let's look at some examples – first of a textbook that doesn't include all four types of material and then of a couple of textbooks that do. *Sociology: themes and perspectives* by Michael Haralambos and others is a massively successful textbook. In the preface to the fourth edition the authors note that the first three editions sold more than half a million copies. The book is an example of a very rare breed, namely the textbook that works successfully with both high-school and college students. Yet, for all its success, the book does not address all kinds of learners equally.

To see how this is so, let us consider Haralambos' chapter on education. There is a considerable amount of discursive prose, as might be expected from such section headings as 'Education – a functionalist perspective' and 'Criticisms and evaluation of social democratic theory'. The text is characterised by the frequent use of the word 'thus' to progress or clinch arguments. There is no doubt, therefore, that the book provides plenty of material for students who learn well through abstract conceptualisation.

In addition to discursive prose, the chapter provides plenty of case studies. These do not, however, always provide for students who tend to learn through concrete experience as well as one might expect. The studies tend to be of research projects, rather than of, say, particular people in (or places of) education. They tend to be summarised rather abstractly, without much actual quotation. Nevertheless, they do present some empirical examples – and quotations from the actual research projects are used occasionally. The chapter might not communicate to students who prefer to learn through concrete experience quite as well as it does to students who learn through abstract conceptualisation, but it does address both types of student a good deal.

Less well off are students who prefer to learn through reflection or active experimentation. One looks in vain for material aimed explicitly at helping readers to reflect on their own educational experience. Similarly, there is no material designed to encourage students either to go out and discover more about the educational context (school, college or distance-learning course) that they are working in or to think how that context could be altered or improved. Given that virtually every one of the half million or more readers of this book will have been in an educational setting when they studied the book, this seems a wasted opportunity.

The success of *Sociology: themes and perspectives* has been so considerable that a teacher of the courses on which it is used might feel discouraged from ever attempting to write a textbook to compete against it. Yet an evaluation of the learning styles implicit in the book's design shows that some types of learner are rather neglected. By no means all students who opt for sociology courses learn best through abstract conceptualisation and concrete experience alone. This suggests that there would be a market for an alternative textbook that did more to include students who rely on the other styles of learning – or that Haralambos could boost his sales still further by doing the same.

My first example of a book that does incorporate all four types of learning material is *An Introduction to Counselling* by John McLeod. Let's look at the first chapter as an example. This chapter, entitled 'An introduction to counselling' begins:

> Paula had been driving her car. Her friend, Marian, was a passenger. Without any warning they were hit by another vehicle. The car spun down the road and Paula thought, 'This is it.'

This turns out to be one of three case studies with which the reader is presented straightaway. The case studies are followed by a section entitled 'What is counselling?' This uses discursive prose to discuss various definitions of counselling that have been proposed. Within the first few pages, then, McLeod has provided opportunities to learn through both concrete experience and abstract conceptualisation.

At the end of the chapter he provides 'topics for reflection and discussion'. The first begins:

> Read through the three definitions of counselling presented on page 3. Do they capture the meaning of counselling, as you understand it?

This explicitly asks readers to relate the abstract material that they have just read to their prior learning and experience. In other words, it is a reflective task.

The last task in this chapter begins:

> Generate a list of all the different forms of 'counselling', defined as widely as possible, that are available in the city or community where you live.

This moves readers away from reflection and towards doing something new. In doing so, it involves them in active experimentation. Thus, by the end of the first chapter, McLeod has presented the reader with an opportunity to learn through all four of the modes that we have discussed above.

For a second example of material that successfully incorporates these four types of learning, I have chosen a passage from *The English Studies Book* by Rob Pope. This book is aimed primarily at undergraduate students of English and related subjects. The passage I have chosen to analyse is about seven pages long and deals with two ways of criticising literature, namely 'practical criticism' and 'New criticism'. It consists of the following elements:

1. A historical and theoretical account of these types of literary criticism;
2. Instructions on how to put these forms of criticism into practice;
3. Three sustained examples of this kind of criticism in practice (discussing passages of poetry, prose and drama);
4. Suggested activities and discussion points.

Element (1) obviously provides the material based on abstract conceptualisation. (2) provides the opportunity for active experimentation: it suggests that the reader tries out these methods of criticism on various pieces of literature. For example, one of the instructions reads:

> Concentrate on short unidentified texts, preferably poems and extracts from novels or short stories, and

ask people to 'comment freely' upon them. On the basis of the ensuing discussion or short comments in writing, try to pick out insensitive, clichéd and 'stock' responses. Aim to cultivate greater 'critical discrimination' and 'literary judgement'.

Note that Pope's use of phrases such as 'try to' and 'aim to' is ideally suited to a passage designed to promote active experimentation.

Element (3) provides concrete experience through case study. (4) provides the opportunity for reflection. For example, one of the activities that Pope suggests in (4) reads:

> <u>Attempt a New Critical analysis of an advert, a news report, a transcript of an interview, a soap opera script.</u> How far do you get? What problems do you encounter?

Although the first sentence of this quotation merely sets up another opportunity for active experimentation, the second and third sentences require the reader to *reflect* on the activity.

Although we have looked at only one section of *The English Studies Book*, Rob Pope has been careful to provide this kind of range of material throughout the book. As a result he has produced a book that will work for many different kinds of reader.

The message is clear: by remembering to include a range of material aimed to suit all kinds of learning style, you will maximise the chances of your textbook succeeding. Many authors, of course, do not concern themselves with questions of learning style. Instead, they cover the material required by their subject in the way that it has always been done, simply trying to do it a little bit better or make their treatment more up to date than the last book. These authors might be very competent, they might even be very successful (like Haralambos) – but they are missing a trick.

5. Structuring Your Material

The single most important point about structure when you are writing a textbook is to keep your eye on the big picture. That is, think, as you write each passage, how it contributes to the chapter that it is a part of. And think, as you write each chapter, how it contributes to the overall shape and pattern of the book.

Authors often fail to do this. It is not difficult to see why. It is very easy to become preoccupied with ensuring that you cover all the ground and that every passage you write is correct. Because of these preoccupations a book can lose balance: the links between passages may be awkward or unclear and the book as a whole offers no clear vision of its subject. Reading such a book can feel like going on a car journey with a bad driver: the reader lurches from one passage to another as if the writer is having difficulty with the gears. Alternatively, it can feel as though whenever the writer introduces a new topic, he or she is saying, 'Oh, and another thing…' Material amassed in this way is difficult both to understand and to remember.

One way to avoid such problems is simply to bear in mind the kind of thing a textbook is. According to Nik Chmiel (in an article in the *THES*), a good textbook:

> is like a good party host: it should introduce you to the crowd, be sensitive to who you are, think of who you would most like to meet, and give you some background on them. At the end, you will know a little about many of the guests and have talked to some of them at length.

Chmiel's party metaphor brings out two key elements of structure in textbooks. First, the writer needs to be selective – although he or she includes a mass of material ('the crowd'), detailed ('at length') discussion is provided of only the most interesting, influential or exciting content. Second, the writer makes all of these decisions relative to the level the reader is working at: in this way he or she is 'sensitive' to the reader's situation.

For these reasons, Chmiel's party metaphor provides an evocative image to keep in mind whenever you are pondering the overall structure of your textbook. But unless you are an extremely gifted organiser of prose, you are likely to also need some more precise techniques for helping you to structure your material. This chapter provides three (not necessarily compatible) techniques.

Progression

The first method for organising material requires a short detour through educational theory. Although the theory might sound somewhat abstract at first, it is worth making this detour because it provides a very powerful way of organising material.

The method is based on a model devised by Jim Cummins of the University of Toronto. Whilst researching the education of bilingual students, he noticed that some students use English well for everyday purposes but not for academic purposes. He also noticed the teachers of these students inferred from their lack of proficiency in academic uses of language that the students were not very intelligent. Cummins realised that this was often not the case.

In order to explain the situation, Cummins devised a simple educational model in the form of a chart with two axes. On the vertical axis he measured educational tasks according to the cognitive demands that they made on the student. Tasks which made low cognitive demands on students would be placed towards the bottom of the axis, whilst cognitively demanding tasks would be placed towards the top.

In distinguishing tasks according to the cognitive demands that they make, Cummins was doing what most teachers do – even though teachers tend to use words like 'easy' and 'difficult' rather than phrases such as 'cognitively undemanding' and 'cognitively demanding'. The reason Cummins avoided terms like 'easy' and 'difficult' was that he realised that the question of how easy or difficult a student found a task depended on more than just the cognitive demands made by that task. That is, a student given two tasks that are equally demanding cognitively may find one easier than the other. This is because, in assessing the ease or difficulty of a task, there is a second dimension to be considered.

This second dimension measures how contextualised a task is. This dimension provides the horizontal axis on Cummins' chart. Before looking at the chart itself, it is helpful to look at an example of what is meant by 'contextualisation'. Take, as an example, two students of politics, one of whom is asked, out of the blue, 'What is "sovereignty"?' The other is given a paragraph from a political article in which the word sovereignty is used. After reading the paragraph, the teacher says 'What do you think the writer means by that word?' In these circumstances we would say that the first student's task was much less contextualised than the second. Educational activities that resembled the first task we would place towards the 'decontextualised' end of the axis, whilst activities such as the latter would be placed nearer the 'contextualised' end.

We now have two axes on which to distinguish educational activities – one to distinguish the degree of cognitive demand made by an activity and one to distinguish the degree of contextualisation. Fig. 5.1 shows how, by putting the two axes together, we can represent Cummins' model as a chart.

So far this model might not sound very useful. Its language is rather abstract ('cognitively demanding', 'decontextualised' and so on) and the model was designed specifically to analyse the long-term development of bilingual learners. With a little more explanation, however, this model becomes a very practical and beautifully simple tool for textbook authors writing for any audience.

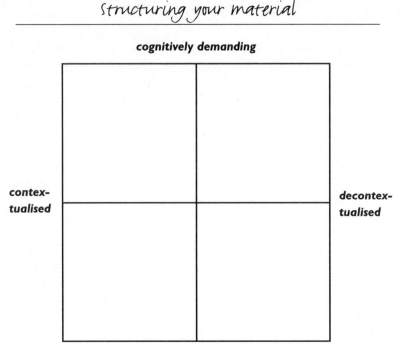

cognitively demanding

contex-
tualised

decontex-
tualised

cognitively undemanding

Fig. 5.1: Cummins' model

Consider some of the learning tasks commonly required in education:

1. Arguing a case using evidence persuasively
2. Comparing and contrasting
3. Describing observations
4. Summarising
5. Retelling
6. Making deductions

Where would these activities fit onto Cummins' chart? Consider the vertical axis first. Activities (3) and (5) are usually not very demanding cognitively. Typically they require little invention or imagination and can be achieved with the use of simple sentence forms. Activities (2) and (4) tend to be cognitively more demanding. Comparing and contrasting are usually more taxing than merely describing, because they require the identification of relations between items. Summarising is usually more taxing than retelling because the former involves selection of material: the pupil has to identify the gist of what he or she is summarising.

How contextualised are these activities? In fact, all four tend to depend very much on context. Usually the subject matter that the pupil has to describe, retell, summarise or compare and contrast is immediately or recently present: pupils describe this story or summarise that painting. In contrast, the activities that we have not yet considered – (1) and (6), both of which are usually fairly obviously demanding in cognitive terms – tend to be decontextualised. The process of deduction – of logically deriving one thing from another – involves moving away from a particular context (the clues left by a murderer, for example) to something new (the solution of the murder mystery). Similarly, arguing a case based on evidence involves taking particular pieces of evidence and marshalling them to do something new.

We can allocate these activities to different quadrants on Cummins' chart as shown in Fig. 5.2.

This model can be used to describe the typical ideal learning path for students. We can summarise this with the following generalisations:

1. Activities that would fall into the bottom right-hand quadrant (i.e. cognitively undemanding, decontextualised activities) are usually a waste of time and should be avoided.
2. Students tend to begin their learning in the bottom left-hand quadrant (i.e. with cognitively undemanding, contextualised tasks).
3. Examination questions and other formal assessment tasks often belong to the top right-hand quadrant (i.e. cognitively demanding, decontextualised tasks).
4. It follows from (2) and (3) together that the major task for instruction is to develop students from the bottom left-hand quadrant to the top right-hand one.
5. According to Cummins and his followers, this is usually best done by developing students through activities from the top

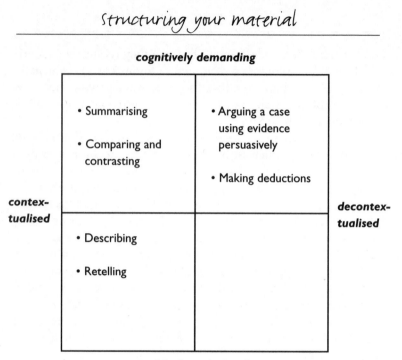

cognitively demanding

• Summarising
 	
• Comparing and
  contrasting
	• Arguing a case
	  using evidence
	  persuasively
	
	• Making deductions

• Describing • Retelling	

contextualised — *decontextualised*

cognitively undemanding

Fig. 5.2: Typical learning activities

left-hand quadrant (i.e. cognitively demanding, contextualised activities). In other words, the degree of cognitive demand made on students should be increased *before* the degree of contextualisation is reduced.

6. It follows from (2), (3) and (5) that the ideal learning path for students tends to be that which takes them first from the bottom left-hand quadrant to the top left and *then* to the top right.

Before applying these points to the construction of textbooks, let's look at a curricular example. Consider a group of high-school students learning about Marlowe's famous play, *Doctor Faustus*. They might start by being given a summary of the plot of the play and some pictures of various incidents in it. Their task would be to use the summary to help them put the pictures into a sequence. This task is contextualised: the students are given the plot summary of a particular play rather than, say, an account of the Faust myth in general. It is also cognitively fairly undemanding: they are being asked only to sequence the pictures, rather than, say, write text to accompany them or suggest alternative ways of sequencing them. This task would, therefore, fall into the bottom left-hand quadrant.

Once students are able to do such tasks, they are ready for cognitively more demanding tasks. For example, they might be given some quotations from the play together with some statements about the characters and asked to decide for each quotation which character is either speaking or being described. This task is still contextualised (they are not, for example, being asked to invent characters on the basis of the quotations alone), but most students would find the connections they have to make more demanding cognitively. This, therefore, is a top left-hand quadrant task.

Once students are able to do these tasks, they are ready for less contextualised tasks. They could, for example, be given extracts from key scenes and asked to guess what happens in between. Here, students are being asked to supply for themselves parts of the context that are missing. Another task they might be given is to decide how inevitable Faustus's downfall is or how much he is to blame. These tasks are both more demanding cognitively and less contextualised than those given above. They belong, therefore, in the top right-hand corner.

Case study

Having considered how Cummins' model applies to curricular activities, let's now look at how it can be applied to the construction of textbooks. I will use as an example a chapter from *Introduction to English Language* by N. F. Blake and Jean Moorhead. This book is written for upper high school and introductory undergraduate courses. The fifth chapter, entitled 'Applying language study to texts', consists of:

1. An introduction;
2. A consideration, with fairly brief examples, of how the style

of texts (ranging from recipes to novels) varies according to
their purpose (to instruct, to entertain and so on);
3. Detailed and sustained analyses of several texts, bringing out
many of their distinctive linguistic features;
4. The provision of six texts for readers to analyse themselves.

In some ways this chapter does follow the ideal learning path
identified by Cummins. The introduction (1) helps to establish a
high degree of contextualisation by relating the chapter explicitly
to previous chapters. The consideration of the style of texts
according to purpose (2) also contextualises points for the reader
by beginning with familiar examples. For example, the section
that describes the style of instructional texts begins with a text
that (as the authors of the textbook note) we have all seen on the
label of a medicine bottle: 'Take one tablet three times a day after
meals'. They follow this with another frequently encountered
instruction: 'Apply polish with a soft brush'. The discussion here
is also cognitively fairly undemanding (at least in relation to the
likely educational level of any reader of the book). It restricts
itself to a consideration of one type of text at a time and, when
it moves onto texts that might cause difficulty (an extract from a
car repair manual, for example) it always explains the source of
that difficulty. For these reasons we might say that the first two
sections of the chapter belong to the bottom left-hand quadrant
of Cummins' model: the material is cognitively undemanding
and contextualised.

When the chapter moves onto detailed and sustained analyses
of texts (3) the cognitive demands on the reader increase. Several
more areas of linguistics are introduced. The analysis of each
text no longer focuses solely on the purpose for which that text
was written. Consequently, the analyses tend to work on a number of different levels. However, although the cognitive demand
on readers has increased, the degree of contextualisation remains
high. The analysis of poetry, for example, concentrates strongly
on the particular poem that is printed in full, rather than on, say,
genres of poetry. Points in the analysis about poetic language are
related explicitly to the text of the poem. Thus the third section
of the book belongs to the top left-hand quadrant of the
Cummins' model: cognitively demanding but contextualised.

In the last section (4) the degree of contextualisation is reduced. The reader is given some texts that the authors have not analysed and invited to 'look for the effects produced by the lexis and meanings, grammatical features, structure, figurative language and other linguistic ways in which the writer tries to influence the reader's response'. In this way readers are invited to develop their understanding of linguistic concepts (such as 'lexis') without the authors' own comments on the texts. In other words, the readers are invited to fill in the context themselves. Thus the final section belongs to the top right-hand quadrant of Cummins' model: the material is cognitively demanding and decontextualised.

On the basis of the above discussion we can plot the progress of the chapter as shown in Fig. 5.3.

cognitively demanding

Section 3 • Demanding: multi-level analysis • Contextualised: analysis restricted to those texts provided for the reader	**Section 4** • Demanding: multi-level analysis • Decontextualised: reader has to provide analysis
Sections 1 and 2 • Undemanding: single level of analysis • Contextualised: familiar texts used	

**contex-
tualised** (left) **decontex-
tualised** (right)

cognitively undemanding

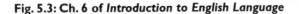

Fig. 5.3: Ch. 6 of *Introduction to English Language*

Although, from Cummins' point of view, the design of the chapter appears to be ideal, in fact the readers' path could have been made even smoother. For example, the texts that are analysed in section (2) tend to be very short (often consisting of single sentences, as in the example of 'Take one tablet three times a day after meals'). My guess is that the authors chose very short texts because they wanted to keep things simple at this stage of the chapter and assumed that short texts are simpler than long ones. If so, this is a classic case of authors thinking along only one dimension, i.e. degree of cognitive demand. Had they also thought about the degree of contextualisation that they were providing for readers, they would have provided more of a context for the sentence of text that they were going to analyse. From the point of view of Cummins' model, the optimum would have been to provide a complete short text (say a bottle label with three short sentences on it) and then an analysis of one (ideally the middle) sentence. This would have kept the cognitive demands of the passage low whilst providing greater contextualisation.

A second way in which the chapter could have provided readers with a smoother path would have been to ease the transition between sections. For example, when the authors move from section (2) to (3), they both increase the numbers of levels of analysis and introduce the reader to new texts. Had they first introduced the new levels of analysis using some of the same texts and only then introduced new texts, the transition would have been less demanding for the reader. Similarly, in section (4) the reader is moved rather suddenly into analysing unfamiliar texts. Had the authors introduced an additional exercise at the beginning of (4) requiring readers to compare and contrast a new text with one that had been analysed already in (3), the transition towards decontextualised thinking would have been smoother.

Of course, the authors could argue that the inclusion of this kind of extra material would have increased the length of the text and made the book uneconomic. That might well be the case. The point of using Cummins' model, however, is to enable you to make your decision about what to include and what to leave out on a more informed basis.

The role of narrative

Although many textbooks include narrative material – history textbooks, for example, often tell the story of historical events and science and social science textbooks sometimes tell the story of discoveries and inventions – textbooks are not generally associated with narrative. Yet textbooks in all subjects tell – or at least could tell – the story of ideas and relationships between them. Narrative construction, then, provides the second technique that textbook authors can use to help structure their material.

It is helpful at this point to consider the work of the Canadian educationalist, Kieran Egan. Egan is particularly impressed by the power of stories. He argues that teachers can improve the way they present material to students by shaping their material in the way that storytellers do.

As a first step, Egan has attempted to describe the way in which stories work on our minds. He points out that:

1. The power of stories over even young children often derives at least in part from the fact that stories typically handle abstract themes (loyalty, for example, or courage).
2. These themes often present themselves in stories through tensions or clashes between opposites (loyalty and betrayal, for example, or courage and cowardice).
3. The feature that often provides a story with a sense of an ending is that the tension between these opposites is resolved (or at least mediated) in some way. One idea might triumph over another, for example; or two ideas might be combined; or they might be replaced by a third idea.
4. This movement in stories from opposites to resolution or mediation resembles the way we learn other things. For example, when it comes to learning about temperature, it seems that children learn the opposites first (hot and cold) and then learn the mediating term 'warm' (and then learn to mediate between 'warm' and 'cold' with the concept 'cool').

All this might sound rather far removed from the business of writing a textbook, yet Egan's theory has very practical implications for the ways in which we instruct students. He suggests that, when a teacher is planning to teach a topic, he or she should identify which set of opposites are most important in that topic. The teacher should then begin the lesson as a story-teller would, establishing the clash or tension between those opposites. During the lesson, the teacher should teach the topic through telling the story of how this dramatic clash develops. And the lesson should end with those opposites being resolved or mediated in some way. Egan gives an example of a lesson in English on writing style, in which the teacher develops the conflict between individuality and convention: the lesson ends with students writing letters that resolve the conflict by using letter-writing conventions to express their individuality.

The implication for textbook authors is clear: according to Egan's theory you should structure your chapters so that they begin by identifying a pair of opposites, continue by telling the story of the struggle between them, and end with some form of resolution or mediation between them.

A good example of a non-fiction book that uses this approach is John Eatwell's *Whatever Happened to Britain?* The book deals both with the economic history of modern Britain and with the history of economic thought that has accompanied that history. At the end of the second chapter, Eatwell writes of the debate about Britain's economic history that it 'is really only two-sided. Do markets work to achieve an efficient allocation of resources via the operation of the price mechanism? Or, even in the best of all possible worlds... does the market not work that way?' The whole of the rest of the book presents British economic history in the light of the struggle between these two views of market forces. I don't know whether Eatwell has ever heard of Kieran Egan, but his book is a model of how to use Egan's theory to produce clear, readable non-fiction that makes complex material readily accessible.

Though the book is not actually a textbook, it is not difficult to see how Eatwell's schema could be adapted for use in designing an economics textbook. An author writing a chapter on currency markets, for example, could focus on the arguments for and against floating rates of exchange, whilst the chapter on labour economics could focus on arguments for and against government regulation of wages, and so on, with each chapter contributing to a running argument over the adequacy (or otherwise) of free market economics.

Structuring books in this way has one major disadvantage, namely that presenting a subject as the story of two opposing ideas or forces can be very reductive. Not all aspects of a subject will fit equally well into the chosen schema. On the other hand, it is true that in some disciplines certain dualisms are already established as central. One thinks of the way in which such dualisms as freedom/authority, nature/nurture, humanity/environment, the individual/society and idealism/materialism form some of the grand themes in many subjects. It is in these cases that Egan's model is most applicable to textbook construction.

One major advantage of Egan's model is its applicability to problems of political correctness. It used to be easy to write history and social studies textbooks with strong narratives, because those subjects often used to concentrate on small, fairly homogenous, élites who shared common experiences. Now, there is much more emphasis on writing inclusively. Todd Gitlin, for example, has described the way that Gary Nash wrote a series of social studies textbooks for Houghton Mifflin. Nash attempted to include the experiences of such diverse groups as Native Americans, African Americans, Hispanics and Chinese Americans. The price that Nash paid was the loss of what Gitlin calls a 'master narrative' ('grand narrative' would have been more politically correct).

The texts:

> Frequently interrupt their master narrative for snippets of social history. They indicate what women were doing. They pause to tell stories about the people who were not movers and shakers... History from above rolls forward with seeming relentlessness. History from below is always stopping, retracing its steps, moving sideways, shifting back and forth, pausing to say 'meanwhile' and 'despite'.

Gitlin adds that 'the books' thematic disjointedness is embodied in, and intensified by, their format':

> There are too many color patches, too many little synopses and boxes. They don't flow easily...The master text is frequently broken up by tinted paragraphs of quotations. The 'narrative' that starts each lesson runs no longer than two paragraphs...before generalizations kick in.

A narrative of ideas, using Egan's model, might well have provided Nash with an alternative to the narrative of events that he found unworkable. He could, for example, have narrated each ethnic group's experience in terms of dualities such as freedom/authority or humanity/environment.

Alternative reading paths

So far I have assumed that all readers are following the same reading paths, i.e. that they are reading the material in the order in which it is printed, from front to back and from top to bottom. Within subsections of chapters, it is probably fair to assume that this is in fact what most readers do (although there is a fair amount of dipping and skipping). Many readers also read whole chapters sequentially, though not necessarily in one sitting – and no doubt there is again a good deal of skipping. At the level of the whole book, there are fewer readers who read sequentially. Factors such as the shape of the courses that the readers are following tend to intervene.

Textbook authors need to accept that, although they can suggest how their books might best be read, they cannot control readers. Consider these instructions to the readers of *An Introduction to Positive Economics* by Richard G. Lipsey:

> It is usually a good idea to read a chapter quickly in order to see the general run of the argument and then to re-read it carefully, making sure that the argument is understood step-by-step. You should be prepared at this stage to spend a very long time on difficult

sections...At various stages you are asked to put the book down and think out the answer to the problem for yourself before you read on: <u>you should never read on without attempting to do what is asked</u>. You should also make your own glossary of technical terms, committing the definitions to memory...After the book has been read in this detailed manner, it should be re-read fairly quickly from cover to cover. (*p. xv*)

I wonder how many of Lipsey's numerous readers have ever followed this advice. Indeed, I wonder whether any reader has ever obeyed all these instructions. Since they come in the introductory section of the book I would guess that many readers simply skipped over Lipsey's instructions altogether. When I read the book I found myself rebelling a little: aren't I allowed to make some decisions for myself? I even find myself wondering whether Lipsey's bossiness is provided to cover up for deficiencies in the text: need the 'difficult sections' be quite so difficult? If a glossary is so important, couldn't he have provided one? *An Introduction to Positive Economics* has been a superbly successful textbook, but I doubt that the passage above contributed much to its success.

One factor that discourages sequential reading is the influence of electronic text. The more our reading habits are shaped by hypertext, the more likely we are to see ourselves as free to jump around between sections of a text and the less likely we are to follow any pre-ordained path for any length of time.

There are two ways in which a textbook author can accommodate non-sequential reading habits in the design of the book. The first is to propose alternative reading paths. For example, you can use the introduction to indicate which chapters assume knowledge of other chapters. Supposing, for example, that your book has ten chapters of which the first three establish the central concepts on which the other seven depend: in that case you can recommend that the reader begins with the first three chapters and then selects chapters in any order.

The most obvious case for specifying alternative reading paths is when a book covers more than one syllabus. Take as an example a textbook that has ten chapters and is used on, amongst others, courses following two syllabuses, (A) and (B). Perhaps syllabus (A) does not require knowledge of the material in Chapter 4, whereas syllabus (B) requires knowledge of the material in Chapter 4 but not of the material in Chapter 7. And perhaps in syllabus (B) the material in Chapter 6 is tested in the same exam paper as the material in Chapter 9 and so it would help the reader to read those two chapters together. In such cases, there is a clear case for providing three contents pages. The first would be the conventional one, listing the chapters in the order in which they appeared in the book. The second would list the chapters in the order in which a candidate for syllabus (A) should read them, with Chapter 4 (the non-required material) given at the bottom under 'additional reading'. The third would list the chapters in the order in which a candidate for syllabus (B) should read them, with Chapter 7 given at the bottom and Chapter 9 inserted between Chapters 6 and 8.

A good example of the provision of alternative reading paths is provided, strangely enough, in another book by Richard Lipsey: *An Introduction to a Mathematical Treatment of Economics*, co-authored with G. C. Archibald. The authors of this book realised from their own teaching experience at the London School of Economics that there would be two types of reader for their book: first, readers who had studied some economics at university but who had given up mathematics at school at the age of sixteen and, second, students who had more advanced mathematics and wanted to see how that subject could be applied to economics. To cater for both types of students they devised a book in which the first few chapters would explain basic mathematical concepts and the rest of the book would alternate between chapters explaining mathematical concepts and chapters that applied those concepts to economics. This is the advice they give:

> At the beginning we assume practically no mathematical background. Students may start reading the mathematics chapters at the point appropriate to their previous training, but they should not skip any of the applications chapters. (*p. 10*)

And

> To students with substantially more mathematics
> than O-Level [i.e. the exam then sat by school students
> at the age of sixteen]: You will find the first math-
> ematical chapters, especially Chapters 2 and 4, tedious
> and unnecessary. You should either skip such chapters
> completely or read them very rapidly. In some topics,
> however, we do go well beyond the standard A-level
> syllabus [i.e. the exam sat by school students at the
> age of 18], and if you wonder if we have any new
> mathematics to teach you at all, you should sample
> Chapter 10 immediately. (*p. 14*)

The second, more radical, response to non-sequential reading
is to structure the book to resemble hypertext. It is useful here
to look again at *The English Studies Book* as an example. In an
introductory section entitled 'What the book is about and how
to use it' the author's instruction is simply, 'Don't aim to read
it straight through from cover to cover'. To help the reader to
jump around within the text, he provides:

1. A glossary – so that the reader can discover the meaning
   of key terms without having to read them in certain
   chapters.
2. A cross-referencing system involving the use of upper-case
   letters, asterisks and bold prints to indicate to readers where
   in the book they can find fuller explanation of terms that
   they encounter whilst reading a passage of their choice. For
   example, if the reader encounters a word in bold, it means
   there is a passage in Section Three of the book that explains
   or discusses that term.
3. The use of short numbered sections, with questions and
   reading lists immediately afterwards (rather than at the end
   of chapters) so that they can be studied independently of
   succeeding sections.
4. A detailed index with bold print to indicate the main
   discussions of each term and with cross-references to other
   terms in the index.

The advantage of these features is the flexibility that they provide. In particular, it allows lecturers to fit the book to their existing courses – a major consideration for a book to get adopted onto reading lists. In the area which *The English Studies Book* covers (which includes such heterogeneous subjects as literary studies, English language, media studies, cultural studies and so on), this is probably the only way in which a textbook can succeed.

The disadvantages, however, are the loss of sustained argument and the risk of overelaborate design features that are expensive to edit and which can confuse or annoy readers. Rob Pope's editor, Moira Taylor, has already decided to simplify the design features when *The English Studies Book* moves into a second edition. In most subjects, the use of all of these features in combination is probably unnecessary and even undesirable. Yet as reading habits become increasingly influenced by the experience of hypertext and as writers become more used to writing hypertext, such features of textbook design are likely to become standard.

Case study

As a way of bringing together the various ideas outlined above, let's look at *Geography* by Peter Haggett. In the preface Haggett tells us that 'Geographers are concerned with the structure and interaction of two major systems: the ecological system that links people with their environment, and the spatial system that links one region with another in a complex interchange of flows.' We can see here the potential for the kind of narrative based on opposites envisaged by Kieran Egan. Such a narrative is very evident in various parts of the book. For example, Haggett outlines the first two of the five main parts of *Geography* as follows:

> Part One, 'The Environmental Challenge,' presents a geographer's view of the uncertain planetary environment in which the human population has evolved and now lives at ever-increasing densities. Part Two, 'Human Ecological Response,' takes up the two-

> pronged response of people to the environmental
> challenge: adaptation of the environment and human
> adaptation to the environment. (*pp. 13–14*)

The phrase 'two-pronged response' virtually guarantees some
form of narrative developing between the two forces he identifies. If we then turn to Chapter 8 ('Pressures on the Ecosystem'),
we find plenty of evidence of this. The chapter begins with a
brief discussion of mercury poisoning suffered by the residents
of the fishing village of Minimata, Japan in 1953. Next comes a
section entitled 'Intervention: Benign or Malign?' which effectively provides a framework for the narrative of interaction
between humans and the environment that runs through the
rest of the chapter. The narrative is developed in three sections
that examine the impact of human intervention at low, medium
and high densities respectively. Admittedly, most of this narrative is rather one-sided (as the chapter title rather suggested).
At the end of the chapter the question 'benign or malign'
resurfaces when, for example, Haggett points out 'it would be
misleading, however, to regard thermal pollution of streams as
only harmful' (p. 186). Haggett provides a conclusion to this
carefully shaped chapter by returning finally to the example of
Minimata. Haggett is a literary-minded craftsman and his
decision to structure much of the book around the story of two
competing forces surely helps to account for its success.

It is illuminating too to analyse *Geography* in the light of
Cummins' model. Take, for example, the first chapter, 'On the
Beach'. Haggett begins by considering a crowd of people on a
beach. He outlines the reactions that geographers might have
to it. They would, for example, be likely to 'try to pin down
exactly where events were occurring in space' (i.e. the space of
the beach). For an advanced level book this provides a cognitively undemanding beginning, dealing with basic questions. It
also provides a highly contextualised opening by restricting the
discussion to a beach (which is contextualised further with a
photograph).

Haggett continues the discussion by considering the theme
of diffusion. This he does by describing the pattern of people
arriving and staying on, and then leaving, a beach in the course

of a day. Here he has moved to a cognitively more demanding topic, i.e. one that includes time and change. By using the example of the beach, however, he keeps the discussion contextualised.

From there he moves to a discussion of scale. He does this by imagining a series of photographs. The first is of a couple on the beach. As the camera moves away, the couple becomes part of the crowd. As the camera moves still further away, the crowd becomes too small in scale to be visible. By the final shot the camera has moved away from the earth's surface altogether and a good part of globe itself is visible. This allows Haggett to consider the world itself as a beach, i.e. as space in which, as on the beach at the opening of a chapter, questions of location and diffusion can be studied. It is difficult to think of either a better or more literal example of a textbook author, having first increased the cognitive demands of the discussion, then decontextualising (or generalising) the discussion too.

Haggett also provides alternative reading paths through his book. In an appendix entitled 'Using the Book in Introductory Courses' Haggett explains how to use the book on courses of different length (ranging from ten to twenty weeks) and made up of various modules (cultural/human geography, economic geography and so on). A diagram shows lecturers for each course which chapters to omit, which to study briefly and which to study in-depth. In the 1970s, when this book was first published, such flexibility was more novel and more radical than it would be today.

Haggett's means of structuring material in this book is very deliberate and explicit. By combining elements of the kind of progression advocated by the Cummins' model with the kind of narrative structure advocated by Egan, Haggett managed to create a new and very successful kind of geography textbook. Of course, something of the overall design of the book is lost as soon as one permits or encourages readers to choose alternative paths, though Haggett is fairly relaxed about this:

> In any book, chapters have to be arranged in a linear (and hopefully logical) sequence. The material in this book has, however, a much more complex structure,

and the sequence of chapters represents only one of many possible compromises. Indeed, the twenty-five chapters could be arranged in more than a billion different ways! (*p. 618*)

The reason that Haggett can be so relaxed is that, as the descriptions of his first and eighth chapters have indicated, the structure *within* chapters is extremely clear and robust.

Conclusion

The concern of this chapter has been to suggest ways in which material can be structured so that a textbook becomes more than a sum of its parts. Three very different (and not necessarily compatible) ways of providing structure have been suggested – the use of Cummins' and Egan's models and the provision of alternative reading paths, most notably through the printed equivalent of hypertext links. Which method an author chooses will depend in part on the subject matter and in part on the author's own preferences. All such methods, however, offer two advantages: (i) when authors are aware of their methods and understand them, they make textbook design and composition, with all the attendant choices over what to include, what to exclude and what to put where, easier; and (ii) they make the resultant book both more readable and more comprehensible. These advantages are not insignificant.

6. Readability

In Chapter 1, I said that successful textbooks need to be clear, pitched at the right level, and organised. I might just as well have said that they need to be readable. Nobody, of course, would quarrel with, or even be surprised by, such a claim. It does, however, lead to two questions that do need discussion, namely what exactly is readability and how do we assess it? This chapter answers those questions. The next chapter will show how you can then write your text as readably as possible.

Assessing readability through common sense

The first way of examining readability involves little more than a structured application of common sense. Simply take any passage from a textbook and analyse it under the following four headings:

1. Verbal difficulties
2. Difficulties arising from sentence construction
3. Conceptual difficulties
4. Design difficulties

Let me explain these headings a little before applying them. By verbal difficulty, I mean difficulties for the reader arising from the author's choice of words. These might arise from an author's use of polysyllabic words, or unfamiliar (or even obscure) words, or vague words – or words that are just wrong.

By difficulties with sentence construction, I mean difficulties that arise from the way in which words have been arranged into sentences (or, at least, difficulties arising from the way in which words relate to one another). These might arise from an author writing sentences that are too long, too complex, or just poorly constructed.

'Conceptual difficulties' means difficulties arising from those concepts or ideas being discussed or assumed by an author, regardless of the words in which they are expressed. For example, some works of philosophy by writers such as Bertrand Russell and A. J. Ayer are renowned for their clarity, yet the very nature of their subject matter means that some readers will nevertheless find their work difficult to understand.

By design difficulties we mean difficulties arising from such matters as size or type of font, layout on the page, unclear diagrams and so on.

To see how this taxonomy of reading difficulties helps, let's consider a passage from *An Introduction to Counselling* by John McLeod. The tenth chapter is entitled 'Understanding theoretical diversity: brand names and special ingredients'. Early in the chapter McLeod includes a section entitled 'Brand names and special ingredients' in which he asks why there are so many different types of counselling ('person-centred', 'psychodynamic' and so on). The first answer that he gives is that in counselling, as in the automobile industry, market forces encourage a variety of brands to develop. The section begins:

> One way of interpreting theoretical diversity in counselling is in commercial terms. It can be argued, following the 'non-specific' hypothesis, that all counsellors and therapists are offering clients the same basic product. The exigencies of the market place, however, mean that there are many pressures leading in the direction of product diversification. It is obvious to anyone socialized into the ways of the market economy that in most circumstances it is not a good idea merely to make and sell 'cars' or 'washing powder'. Who would buy an unbranded car or box of detergent? Products which are on sale usually have brand names, which are meant to inform the customer about the quality and reliability of the commodity being sold. To stimulate customer enthusiasm and thereby encourage sales, many products also boast 'special ingredients' or 'unique

selling features', which are claimed to make the product superior to its rivals. (*p. 189*)

What difficulties does this passage present to the reader? I can see three verbal difficulties. The first stems from the phrase 'non-specific hypothesis'. This difficulty arises only because I have taken McLeod's passage out of context: earlier in the chapter it has been explained that the 'non-specific hypothesis' refers to the claim that the value of counselling lies in those features that all types of counselling share. For the purposes of this discussion the phrase can simply be ignored.

A second verbal problem stems from 'exigencies'. Although this word is far from esoteric, neither is it exactly common. It is a fair bet that some of McLeod's readers will be somewhat hazy about its precise meaning. And, in fact, when we look at the precise meaning – my dictionary defines 'exigency' as 'urgent need' or 'emergency' – I am not sure that its nuances are either necessary or helpful in this sentence. Nothing would be lost by replacing 'exigencies of the market place' with 'workings of the market' or 'market forces'. Either phrase would make the passage more accessible.

Another verbal difficulty stems from 'socialized'. Generally speaking, I understand the word 'socialized', but when I read it in the context of this sentence I feel a little perplexed. What exactly does it mean to be 'socialized into the ways of the market economy'? It sounds like the kind of shorthand that two sociologists talking to each other might understand, but which the rest of us might flounder with. In fact, there is no reason why McLeod should even present us with the problem of wondering what 'socialized' means: for the purposes of his argument, all he really needs to say is 'we all know that in a market economy...'

The main difficulty arising from sentence construction stems from the word 'diversification'. The problem is that readers typically find abstract nouns less accessible than the verbs they stem from. If, instead, the sentence said that market forces 'encourage counsellors to diversify their products' or 'encourage the counselling industry to diversify its products', it would be more accessible.

A second syntactical or grammatical difficulty arises from the final clause of the passage. Had McLeod followed the phrase 'unique selling features' with 'that' instead of with a comma followed by 'which', the sentence would have been both more succinct and more focused. He could also have simplified the sentence by omitting the passive construction 'are claimed to make'.

I have, however, been negative enough. There is also some effective writing in the passage. Consider, for example, the directness and clarity provided by the question 'Who would buy an unbranded car or box of detergent?' Consider too the sentence 'Products which are on sale usually have brand names, which are meant to inform the customer about the quality and reliability of the commodity being sold'. There may not be anything outstanding about such a sentence – and perhaps there are some unnecessary words in the final clause – but it surely does its job.

The conceptual difficulty presented by the passage lies in the sophistication (and unfamiliarity) of the idea that schools of counselling operate like commercial brands. McLeod can hardly avoid this difficulty: the idea is the hub of the passage. And, in fact, he does give the reader some help, both by signalling the idea in the passage's heading ('Brand names and special ingredients') and by providing the analogy with cars and detergents.

Design difficulties are usually the responsibility of the publisher rather than the author. In this case, Open University Press has been careful to leave wide margins so that, even though the page is a wide one, the line of print is of standard length. The publisher has also chosen a serif font, which helps to lead the eye from left to right across the page. Both of these features aid readability. On the other hand, the font is perhaps on the small side.

This analysis might seem rather pedantic. Most of the obstacles to readability that I have identified are fairly minor. If, however, such obstacles appear on page after page they have a cumulative effect that makes the task of reading a chapter of, say, a dozen pages off-putting.

Here is the next paragraph of McLeod's text:

This analogy is applicable to counselling and therapy. The evidence on the non-specific hypothesis implies that counsellors and therapists are, like car manufacturers, all engaged in selling broadly similar products. But for reasons of professional identity, intellectual coherence and external legitimacy, there have emerged a number of 'brand name' therapies. The best known of these brand name therapies have been reviewed in earlier chapters. Psychodynamic, person-centred and cognitive-behavioural approaches are widely used, generally accepted and universally recognized. They are equivalent to the Mercedes, Ford and Toyota of the therapy world. Other, smaller, 'firms' have sought to establish their own brand names. Some of these brands have established themselves in a niche in the market place. (*pp. 189–90*)

It might be helpful at this stage for you to analyse the passage yourself under the headings of verbal, grammatical or syntactical, and conceptual difficulties. All I will say is that McLeod should be congratulated for the sentence 'They are equivalent to the Mercedes, Ford and Toyota of the therapy world'. This has the kind of directness and colour that benefits textbook style considerably.

Assessing readability numerically

A second way of assessing readability is through statistical measures. There are various ways of doing this, the simplest of which is to apply what is known as McLaughlin's SMOG formula. This formula, which works on the simple assumption that the more polysyllabic words used in a text, the less readable it becomes, is as follows:

Reading age = 8 + the square root of the number of polysyllabic words

To apply it, count the number of words of three or more syllables in a passage of 30 sentences. For example, the results from the first 30 sentences (ending '...three verbal difficulties') of this chapter are as follows:

Number of words with at least three syllables: 109
Square root of 109 = 10.44
8 + 10.44 = 18.44
Reading age required for reading the passage: 18+ years, i.e. adult

The problem with this formula is that it ignores one of the main determinants of readability, namely the length of sentences. Most readability tests take account of the length of both words and sentences. One such test is the Flesch Reading Ease Test. To conduct this test, select a typical passage of 100 words from the textbook you are assessing and follow the steps below:

1. Count the number of syllables in the passage.
2. Divide the number of syllables by the number of words (i.e. by 100). This gives you the average number of syllables per word.
3. Multiply the average number of syllables per word by 84.6.
4. Count the number of sentences. (Here, this means count the number of full units ending in a full stop, question mark, colon, semi-colon or dash.)
5. Divide the number of words (100) by the number of sentences. This gives you the average number of words per sentence.
6. Multiply the average number of words per sentence by 1.015.
7. Add the total you calculated in (3) to the total you calculated in (6).
8. Subtract the total you calculated in (7) from 206.835. This gives you a readability score. The higher the score, the more readable the passage. Texts that score at least 60 are likely to be written in plain English.

Although this sounds fiddly and a little baffling (why all those strange figures like 206.835?), it is in fact quite easy to operate. Consider, for example, the first 100 words of the passage from McLeod beginning 'This analogy is applicable...' The Flesch test produces the following results:

1. The number of syllables in the first 100 words is 199.
2. The number of syllables divided by the number of words is 1.99.
3. The average number of syllables per word (1.99) multiplied by 84.6 gives a total of 168.354.
4. The number of sentences is 6.6.
5. The number of words divided by the number of sentences is 15.152.
6. The average number of words per sentence (15.152) multiplied by 1.015 gives a total of 15.379.
7. 168.354 + 15.379 = 183.733.
8. 206.835 − 183.733 = 23.102.

This score is low, suggesting that the passage is not very readable. The main reason for this is the frequent use of polysyllabic words such as 'legitimacy' and 'behavioural'.

Now apply the test to the first 100 words of the first passage that I quoted from McLeod (beginning 'One way of interpreting...'). What readability score did you calculate?

The respective scores are:

1. 168
2. 1.68
3. 142.128
4. 5.2
5. 19.23
6. 19.518
7. 161.646
8. 45.189

The advantage of using a statistical test is that it makes it easy for you to compare one text with another. For example, according to the Flesch test, the McLeod passage beginning 'One way of interpreting...' (readability score approximately 45) is significantly more readable than the one beginning 'This analogy is applicable...' (score approximately 23).

Such scores enable authors to identify their least readable passages so that they can try to redraft them. Ask yourself whether, if you were John McLeod, you would rewrite the less readable passage and, if so, how.

Assessing readability through a combination of methods

You should always examine the passage to see whether you think the readability score that you have calculated is reliable. After all, the assumptions on which the Flesch test are based are not always valid: long words are not always less readable than shorter ones and long sentences are not always less readable than shorter ones. The best way to assess readability is to combine the statistical test with the common-sense method outlined above.

To see how this can be done, consider the following passage from *Basic Marketing: principles and practice* by Tom Cannon. This is a successful book and has run to several editions. The passage comes from a chapter entitled 'Marketing research' and comes at the beginning of a section called 'Research in the firm':

> Despite the importance of information to effective marketing, there is a tendency in many firms to narrowly define the role of the market or marketing research department as simply to gather data, and this is a role which has been welcomed by some researchers whose dedication to their methodologies outweighs their desire to make a real contribution to corporate effectiveness.

> Many involved in both marketing and research recognize that this approach diminishes the contribution that research can make to improving the quality of planning and decision-making, as well as more conventional information-gathering to answer more or less urgent questions. In playing this larger part in the firm's activities the fundamental disciplines retain

their importance but become part of a larger system of information and knowledge. (*p. 102*)

The Flesch test produces a readability score of only 8.81. This suggests that the passage is less readable than either of the passages from McLeod. Now let's apply common sense to this finding and ask whether it is reliable, i.e. is the passage really the least readable of the three? I think it is. I was certainly aware whilst reading the Cannon passage that it felt wordy.

Let us, therefore, apply common sense further by asking whether the process of calculating the Flesch score has highlighted the causes of the comparative lack of readability. The average number of syllables per word was 1.74, which is between the averages for the two McLeod passages. The average number of words per sentence is 50, which is much higher than in either of the McLeod passages. Read the Cannon passage again and ask yourself whether the length of sentences causes a problem. I think they do. By the time I reach the clause beginning 'and this is a role' I feel I have read enough for one sentence. I had a similar feeling when I reached 'as well as' in the second sentence.

If we continue to apply the common-sense method, what else does it reveal? First, there are verbal difficulties caused by polysyllabic words and phrases such as 'methodologies' (why not just 'methods'?) and 'corporate effectiveness' – especially when they come towards the end of long sentences.

Second, there are syntactical difficulties caused not just by the length of sentences but also by word placing ('narrowly' is awkwardly placed) and construction ('gathering' would be happier than 'to gather').

When it comes to conceptual difficulty, the interesting point is that the passage need be no more difficult than either of the McLeod passages. Indeed conceptually it is probably the least difficult of the three: all that Cannon is saying in essence is that companies could be more effective if they didn't restrict their marketing departments merely to collecting information.

Unfortunately the publisher has added to the difficulties that Cannon presents to his reader by using longer lines of print and a smaller font than was the case with McLeod.

The combination of running the Flesch test and applying common sense has revealed that Cannon's text (which, I stress, is from a successful book) is unnecessarily difficult for the reader. It has also indicated clear ways of making the passage more readable: break the long sentences into shorter ones; simplify the vocabulary; and polish the word order and sentence construction.

Conceptual difficulties

So far I have said little about conceptual issues in this chapter. The emphasis has been rather on linguistic (verbal, syntactical and grammatical) issues. This is partly because, in effect, conceptual issues have been dealt with in Chapters 4 and 5. Chapter 4 showed how readers benefit from conceptual material being presented in various forms (case studies, discursive prose and so on), whilst Chapter 5 showed how authors can minimise conceptual difficulties through the frameworks that they use to organise material. There is, however, more to be said.

(a) Questions and answers

When I used to teach English literature to senior grades in high school, I had some students who were willing to read literary criticism in order to see what other people had said about the books they were studying. Unfortunately, this reading rarely proved fruitful. When I asked myself why this was so, the main reason seemed to be that the questions the critics were answering (or the problems that they were solving) were different from those that my students were grappling with. As a result, my students were having to read against the grain of the criticism. They had to extract, from passages of literary criticism aimed at answering one kind of question, the answers to their own questions. Such reading is difficult to do. To make matters worse, my students did not always know what questions the critics were themselves trying to answer. The result was usually – and understandably – befuddlement.

To see why this was so, let us consider an example. Here is an extract from the first chapter of *Modern Drama in Theory and Practice* (vol. 1) by J. L. Styan:

> Although the well-made play might introduce some political satire, social criticism or even subtlety of character, any of this was subordinate to the contrivances of the plotting; indeed, in his preface to *La Haine* Sardou confessed that he invented the *scène à faire* first, and then worked out his plot backwards. It is little wonder that characters and situations looked much the same from play to play. Yet it was an immensely successful arrangement, and well into the twentieth century the aspiring playwright could still have found rules for writing a well-made play as laid down by William Archer in his *Play-Making: A Manual of Craftmanship* (1912). (*p. 5*)

This is typical of the kind of passage that my students found profitless. I doubt that much of the difficulty would arise from the language of the passage. The Flesch score for the passage is 49, which indicates that, though demanding, it is more readable than any of the passages that we have considered so far. I suspect that the main difficulty would arise from uncertainty about what kind of question Styan is trying to answer. In fact, Styan is considering how one form of drama ('realism') replaced another form ('the well-made play'). In particular, he is answering the questions:

1. What was the 'well-made play'? (The two paragraphs with which Styan precedes the paragraph quoted here also answer that question.)
2. In particular, what were the characteristic weaknesses of the 'well-made play'?
3. And why did the 'well-made play', for all its weaknesses, survive as a major form of drama for so long?

Had the passage quoted above been preceded by a list of these questions, you would, I suspect, have found it much more readable. In particular, you would be likely to have made more sense of those words ('although', 'indeed' and 'however') that signal the direction of Styan's argument.

I do not want to be unfair to the author here. I have drastically exaggerated the difficulty of his text by quoting a paragraph out of context. In fact, I find the section of which it is a part both well-written and informative. I have removed the paragraph above from the context that Styan gave it simply to demonstrate how much the readability of a passage depends on our knowledge of what questions it is trying to answer. It is easy to see why, when Karl Popper was teaching philosophy, he used to tell his students that the first thing they should do when reading a work of philosophy is to decide what questions the author is trying to answer.

Remember that many readers of textbooks do read passages out of context. Sometimes their teacher recommends that they read only selected pages from a particular book. Sometimes students have to research one particular topic and so gather together a number of textbooks and use the index page to identify only those pages relevant to that topic. Usually such piecemeal reading does not take the extreme form of reading just one paragraph from a book: it is more likely that students will read an individual chapter or a section of that chapter. The textbook author who ensures that chapters and sections begin by clarifying what questions they are considering will provide for such students and, in the process, broaden the market for the book.

(b) Cultural literacy

Lack of clarity about the questions that a text is answering is one cause of conceptual difficulty for readers. Another cause is lack of cultural knowledge on the part of the reader. Consider, for example, an experiment made in 1978 when some college students in America were given a passage beginning:

> When Ulysses S. Grant and Robert E. Lee met in the parlor of a modest house at Appomattox Courthouse, Virginia, on April 9, 1865, to work out the terms for the surrender of Lee's army of Northern Virginia, a great chapter in American life came to a close, and a great new chapter began.

Many students did not understand the passage. One of the main reasons was simply that they did not have the cultural knowledge assumed by the writer.

In his book *Cultural Literacy*, E. D. Hirsch identifies the knowledge that students would need in order to make sense of the passage that began with the paragraph above. They would need to know:

1. America fought a Civil War.
2. The two sides were the Union and the Confederacy.
3. Grant was the chief general for the Union.
4. Lee was the chief general for the Confederacy.
5. The Union won.

Now look at the passage from Styan's book on drama quoted above. The passage rather assumes that the reader will know who Sardou and William Archer are. In fact, by this stage in the book, Styan has already introduced Sardou. William Archer, however, is not properly introduced until a later chapter. The meaning of the passage does not entirely depend on their identity, but a reader who is lacking in confidence might well be troubled by the sense of a knowledge gap.

Such gaps arise because of cultural differences between authors and students. They may belong to different socio-economic or ethnic groups, have different educational backgrounds or simply come from different generations. Gaps are likely to be even greater when a textbook is being used outside its country of origin.

Conclusion

The more readable a textbook is, the more likely it is to be successful. The gist of this chapter is simply that an author is more likely to write readably if he or she understands what readability consists of and how it can be assessed. We have seen, in particular, how readability can be assessed both through the structured application of common sense and statistically – and that the best results come from a combination of the two. We have also seen that readability has several components: in addition to design factors (which are likely to be the concern of the publisher more than the author), readability depends on verbal, syntactical, grammatical and conceptual factors. In the case of the conceptual element of readability, authors should consider what questions a text is trying to answer and what knowledge is assumed by it.

The next chapter will consider how you can use this knowledge to inform the way you write.

7. Language and Style

The previous chapter provided ways of analysing the readability of texts. It pointed to four sources of difficulty for readers: words; sentence construction; concepts; and design. This chapter suggests ways of avoiding or overcoming the first three of these problems. Design issues will be left until Chapter 9.

Using words well

In *The King's English* H. W. and F. G. Fowler offer writers the following guidelines on vocabulary, complete with examples:

1. Prefer the familiar word to the far-fetched (*The Times* once wrote 'Continual vigilance is imperative on the public': the Fowlers suggest that 'We must be ever on the watch' would have been preferable);
2. Prefer the concrete word to the abstract (*The Spectator* once wrote 'No year passes now without evidence of the truth of the statement that...': 'Every year shows again how true it is that...' would have been preferable);
3. Prefer the single word to the circumlocution (an examiner's report once referred to 'fine penmanship in the case of both boys and girls': 'in the case of' could have been replaced by 'by');
4. Prefer the short word to the long (*The Times* once reported that 'On the Berlin Bourse today the prospect of a general strike was cheerfully envisaged': 'faced' would have been preferable to 'envisaged');
5. Prefer the Saxon word to the Romance (*The Guernsey Advertiser* once began a sentence, 'Despite the unfavourable

climatic conditions...': why not just 'Bad as the weather has been...'?).

Although some of their examples now sound dated, the Fowlers' guidelines can still help authors to write more readably, so let us explore some of these guidelines in more detail. The discussion below considers each of the Fowlers' principles in turn except (4), which is subsumed in the others. I will also add one principle of my own.

Prefer the familiar word to the far-fetched
One reason why authors sometimes neglect the more familiar word is the prevalence of jargon. ('Jargon' here means the technical or specialist language of a particular discipline, profession or occupation. For an alternative, now less common, meaning of jargon, see the section on circumlocution below.) Used between two specialists, jargon offers a harmless and concise means of communication. Used in writing for a non-specialist, jargon is opaque and unwelcoming. Gordon Brown, the British Chancellor of the Exchequer, was once ridiculed in the press for referring in a speech to 'neoclassical endogenous growth theory'. Amongst economists that would be a very efficient way to talk, but in a speech intended for a non-specialist public such jargon is ineffective.

Beware when you feel tempted to use jargon. Either avoid it or explain it.

That is easy advice to give, but there is a difficulty: textbook authors tend to be so well acquainted with their subject that they are prone to using jargon unwittingly. A useful preventive measure is to browse occasionally through subject dictionaries, especially those intended for beginners. These will remind you of the types of words that need to be explained to your reader.

Sometimes the reason why authors fail to choose the familiar word in preference to the far-fetched is the attraction of foreign and classical phraseology. Authors who have enjoyed a classical education tend to employ phrases such as 'inter alia' and 'prima facie' without realising that many of their readers will not understand them. There are numerous examples: 'mutatis mutandis', 'ceteris paribus', 'de jure', 'op cit', 'per se' and so on (or 'et cetera'). Similarly, authors who have enjoyed a polyglot education are likely to use such phrases as 'raison d'être', 'dénouement', 'frisson', 'sotto voce', 'Schadenfreude' or 'ennui'. Such phrases have, of course, more or less become part of the English language. The problem is that they have become part of only *some* people's English language. To use them unexplained is, therefore, to cut oneself off from a number of readers.

Fortunately it is not difficult to develop an awareness of the type of words and phrases likely to cause readers problems. Simply browsing through some etymological resources – the *Bloomsbury Dictionary of Word Origins*, for example, or Rosalind Ferguson, *Chambers Dictionary of Foreign Words and Phrases* – will stimulate the necessary sensitivity.

Prefer the concrete word to the abstract
Abstract nouns frequently result from the conversion of verbs. For example, if I were writing (say, in a textbook about education) about the way in which exam boards operate, I might write:

> Exam boards exemplify standards by providing portfolios of students' work for each grade.

Alternatively I might write:

> Exemplification of standards by the exam board is through the provision of portfolios of students' work for each grade.

Here I have converted two verbs ('exemplify' and 'providing') into nouns. In the process of conversion, which is known as nominalisation, I have made the sentence slightly less easy to read. It has become more abstract and the number of syllables has increased. 'Exemplification', for example, has six syllables. This might not matter very much if we are talking about just one sentence, but if this sort of decision is made by an author several times per page then the text will become much less readable.

Since sentences using the verb forms are usually the more readable, one might ask whether there is ever a case for nominalisation. In fact, the relative desirability of noun and verb forms depends on the purpose of the writer. If the main purpose is to register an event, the author would probably prefer the verb form ('The exam board exemplified standards'), perhaps with the addition of an adverb (e.g. 'fully') or an adverbial phrase (e.g. 'by reference to answers from this year's exam'). If his or her main purpose is to provide a full account of a process, he or she is more likely to prefer the noun form: e.g. 'thorough exemplification of standards was provided by reference to answers to this year's exam questions with helpful annotations from the chief examiner'.

Often, however, it is possible to avoid the sentence beginning with the abstract noun by using two or more sentences using the verb form. For example, instead of the sentence beginning 'thorough exemplification of standards was provided' one might write:

> Standards were exemplified thoroughly. This was done by reference to the answers to this year's exam questions...

Sometimes (though not here) the decision to avoid nominalisation by using more than one sentence results in more words being used. One is faced with a trade-off between concision and accessibility.

Prefer the single word to the circumlocution

I mentioned above that 'jargon' has two meanings. The meaning we didn't consider then was defined by the Fowlers as 'the use of long words, circumlocution, and other clumsiness'. It is this meaning that Sir Arthur Quiller-Couch had in mind when he wrote an essay on jargon. In that essay he rewrote the beginning of Hamlet's famous 'To be or not to be' soliloquy as jargon. Here are the lines from Shakespeare:

> To be, or not to be, that is the question:
> Whether 'tis nobler in the mind to suffer

The slings and arrows of outrageous fortune,
Or to take arms against a sea of troubles,
And by opposing end them

(Act III Scene ii)

And here is Quiller-Couch's version:

> To be, or the contrary? Whether the former or the
> latter be preferable would seem to admit of some
> difference of opinion; the answer in the present case
> being of an affirmative or of a negative character
> according as to whether one elects on the one hand to
> mentally suffer the disfavour of fortune, albeit in an
> extreme degree, or on the other to boldly envisage
> adverse conditions in the prospect of eventually
> bringing them to conclusion.

Quiller-Couch's essay, which was published in 1913, retains its relevance. The value of the passage above is that it acts as a kind of touchstone of all that we should try to avoid. To read phrases such as 'would seem to admit', 'in the present case' and 'according as to whether' and see how deadening they are is to inoculate oneself against using such phrases oneself.

Two common causes of circumlocution are euphemism (we speak of people 'passing away', 'going to meet their maker' and so on, rather than dying) and pomposity. The latter is more hazardous for textbook authors. As an example of pomposity, consider a letter that my boss recently received: it said 'I hope this gives you complete data satisfaction' (i.e. 'I hope you have all the information you need'). It is easy, when looking at such examples, to think, 'I would never write like that', yet this kind of pomposity is very common.

It often happens when writers feel superior to their audience, but it also happens, more insidiously, when authors feel insecure, either because they are short of material or they do not have a secure grasp of the subject. The temptation then is for such authors to try to hide these shortcomings (certainly from their readers and perhaps even from themselves). Authors in this position might resort to a pompous tone in the hope that this will create the impression of expertise. The solution is to be scrupulously honest with oneself: if you feel insecure in your understanding of the topic, clarify your understanding rather than bluff.

Circumlocutions often occur in adverbial phrases. 'At this moment in time' is a circumlocution for 'now'; 'until such time as...' may be replaced by 'until'; 'during such time' may be replaced by 'while'. They also occur frequently in verb phrases. In particular, prepositions in verb phrases are often redundant. Consider 'try out', 'comprises of', 'start up' and (perhaps most prevalent of all) 'report back'. Common three-word circumlocutions include 'is supportive of' and 'is protective of'.

Prefer the Saxon word to the Romance

The English lexicon derives from numerous languages. The two most common origins were (i) Saxon (and similar languages from northern Europe) and (ii) Latin and those languages, especially French, that derived from it. Languages in the latter group are known as Romance languages.

English often has two words to describe the same thing, one word being derived from Saxon and the other from a Romance language. Consider, for example, the naughty parts of the body and what one does with them. From Romance languages we have respectable words such as 'penis', 'vagina' and 'copulate'; from Saxon we have ... well, the unprintable ones. Often the use of Romance words can make one sound more educated – the very language of education, e.g. 'curriculum', 'scholar', 'examination' and 'education' itself, have Romance origins. Yet such words are often less accessible and less energetic. Consider, for example, the following versions of the opening lines of a well-known drinking song. First, the more Saxon version:

> Show me the way to go home
> I'm tired and I want to go to bed

Second the Romance:

> Indicate the way to my habitual abode
> I'm fatigued and I wish to retire

95

No prizes for guessing which comes more naturally after a few beers.

Often an author, being highly educated, will deploy a Romance vocabulary automatically, thereby writing text that less educated students might find alien or obscure. Fortunately, one can very rapidly develop a feel for where one's vocabulary is over-dependent on Romance words. Simply skimming through an etymological dictionary or a history of the English language will heighten awareness.

One further principle

The Fowlers should have added a further principle, namely 'Prefer the right word'. This principle sounds banal until we remember the existence of confusables (two or more words that are commonly confused with each other). English has numerous examples: 'affect'/'effect', 'continual'/'continuous', 'effective'/'effectual', 'repetitious'/'repetitive', 'reflective'/ 'reflexive' and so on.

It is useful to develop a personal record of the words that one has trouble with. Whenever you find yourself hesitating between one word and another, make a note of it. It is easy then to consult a dictionary of confusables or troublesome words. It is more important to remember which words are confusables than what the distinctions between the confusables are: provided you do the former, you can rely on reference books to help you with the latter.

Constructing better sentences

Agreement

A common difficulty with sentence construction is lack of agreement between subject and verb. This happens when a singular noun is used with a plural verb or vice versa. The error sounds so obvious that no writer ever believes that he or she is guilty of it, yet it is notoriously easy to make this mistake.

The usual cause of the problem is a phenomenon known as attraction. Consider the following sentence (cited by Ernest Gowers in *The Complete Plain Words*):

> Thousands of pounds' worth of damage have been done to the apple crop.

The subject ('damage') is singular and so the verb should be 'has', but the writer has been misled by the plural noun ('pounds'). In other words, the plural noun has attracted a plural verb.

Now look at the attraction in the following example (also cited by Gowers):

> We regret that assurances given us twelve months ago that a sufficient supply of suitable local labour would be available to meet our requirements has not been fulfilled.

Here the subject ('assurances') is plural but the verb ('has') is singular. The writer has presumably been misled by the presence of the singular noun 'labour' – as, evidently, was the grammar checker on my word processor, which failed to spot the error.

There is one possible exception to the usual requirement of agreement. This is when an author uses 'they' with a singular verb in order to avoid sexism. If one is writing in the singular and wants to avoid writing 'he', there are various solutions. One can change the whole clause into the plural. Or one can use 'one' or 's/he' or 'he or she' as the pronoun. Sometimes, however, none of these solutions seems to fit. In these cases, the best (i.e. least inelegant) solution might be to use 'they' with a singular verb. This is now widely accepted in conversation (indeed, one might say that in certain contexts 'they' is now a singular pronoun). The usage is coming to be accepted in writing, though many publishers are reluctant to permit it in the kind of formal writing that characterises textbooks.

Adverbs

Writers frequently have problems with the positioning of adverbs. This is especially common with 'only'. Gowers gives the following example:

His disease can only be alleviated by a surgical operation

He points out that this could mean either 'Only a surgical operation [i.e. that, and nothing else] can alleviate his disease' or 'a surgical operation can only alleviate [i.e. not entirely cure] his disease'. If in doubt about the placement of adverbs, the best solution is simply to write the sentence and then read it back – or, preferably, ask somebody else to read it – and see whether it is capable of misinterpretation.

Headline phrases
'Headline phrases' are indigestible sequences of words usually caused by the use of a noun form as an adjective. Consider, for example, the following:

WOMEN PRISON BOSSES SEX LETTER SCANDAL

Maybe you understood this sentence straightaway – I had to read it several times before the string of half a dozen noun forms made sense to me.

Inadvertent use of headline phrases is becoming more common in textbook writing, not least because of the increasing use of 'management', 'government' and 'money' as adjectives in preference to 'managerial', 'governmental' and 'monetary'. The best solutions are to use 'of' as a way of breaking up words (e.g. 'boss of prison') and to remember to use adjectival forms (e.g. 'female prison bosses').

Redundancy
Redundancy occurs when words or phrases are used in a sentence without adding anything to its meaning. For example, one of my authors sent me a manuscript with the following (very inelegant) sentence:

A second reason that raising standards is so difficult is due to the fact stated in the previous section, that the school populations are much more diverse than they have ever been before.

98

'Reason' overlaps with 'due to'.

There are two common forms of redundancy. The first is pleonasm, common examples of which include 'added bonus' (a bonus is necessarily something added), 'local derby', 'free gift', 'never ever' (which has for some reason become extremely popular in speech, though not so far in writing) and 'forward planning'. 'Again' is often used pleonastically (as in 'repeat again'), as is 'both' (e.g. 'both A and B are similar' – well, neither A nor B could be similar on its own!). Unless used deliberately for emphasis, 'actually' is usually redundant. Acronyms often become associated with pleonasms, e.g. 'PIN number' (= 'Personal Identification Number number'!) and 'ISA account' (= 'Individual Savings Account account'!).

The second common form of redundancy is padding. In textbooks this occurs most often with phrases such as 'it should be noted that' and 'it is important to bear in mind'. Omitting such phrases usually creates sparer, brisker, prose. One of the reasons that Haralambos is able to cover so much ground in *Sociology: themes and perspectives* is that he writes in a concise style largely devoid of such phrases.

The use of models

So far we have taken a rather negative view of usage. I have concentrated first on problems and only then on the solutions. There is, however, an altogether more positive approach. This is to read examples of well-written textbooks and to use them as models.

The process of learning from models happens partly by infection. The style of well-written texts often simply rubs off on the reader. This is particularly true of their abstract qualities – the reader catches something of the directness, pace and fluency of the writing.

You may find this process of infection sufficient. It might help, however, to supplement it with more conscious study of the best models. Concentrate on textbooks that are pitched at the same level as the one that you are writing. If possible, choose two books with a subject in common so that you can compare and contrast. Your models should not, however, be on the same subject as your own book, because there is a risk of becoming enslaved or intimidated by them. You do, after all, want to preserve the freshness of your own style and approach.

Once you have identified a textbook that you feel is well written, read it by concentrating on the language and craft of the writer rather than on the subject matter. Ask yourself what it is about the writer's handling of language that impresses you.

Often this is difficult to answer for the simple reason that good textbook authors tend to be unobtrusive. Whereas writers of more expressive forms, such as poetry and fiction, are often expected to develop distinctive voices, the main priority for textbook authors is not to allow themselves to come between the reader and the subject matter. Finding how an author succeeds in this can be difficult because it is often a matter of negatives – of not choosing over-elaborate language, of _not_ constructing complex sentences, and so on.

There are, however, various ways of identifying an author's strengths. Find a passage that you feel illustrates your model author at his or her best and try rewriting it. You don't need to rewrite all of it. Try, for example, taking out single words and putting in shadow words as substitutes. If you find that the ones that you have substituted do not work so well, that is a sign that your author is writing precisely. If you compare one of his or her words with one of your less successful substitutes you will be able to identify the nuances that made the original word the right one.

Use the same technique to examine the author's syntax. That is, take one of the author's sentences, write a sentence yourself that is intended to say the same thing and substitute it for the original. If you find that your substitute does not work so well, look back at the original to see what it is that you have lost. Usually this is a matter either of emphasis within the sentence or a question of how the sentence connects with those on either side of it.

Consider too the rhythm of the passages you have chosen to study. We all recognise that rhythm is an important element of such artistic forms as verse, but it also plays an important role in expository prose. This is both because textbooks – or at least parts of them – are sometimes read aloud in classes and because our inner ear responds to rhythm even when we read silently.

It can be hard to detect the rhythm of such prose because it tends to be both less regular and less pronounced than in poetry. The best way to detect it is by reading aloud. Authors who lack a control of rhythm are hard work to read aloud – their text feels clumsy and awkward and the reader can find no pattern – whereas texts in which the rhythm is controlled seem to guide the reader and make the voice glide.

In her classic book, *Becoming a Writer*, Dorothea Brande suggests a more painstaking method for learning from model passages:

> The first sentence [of the text you have chosen as your model] has twelve words; you will write a twelve-word sentence. It begins with two words of one syllable each, the third is a noun of two syllables, the fourth is an adjective of four syllables... etc. Write one with the words of the same number of syllables, noun for noun, adjective for adjective, verb for verb, being sure that the words carry their emphasis on the same syllables as those in the model. By choosing an author whose style is complementary to your own you can teach yourself a great deal about sentence formation and prose rhythm. (*p.100*)

Having considered how to learn from models, let us look at one passage in detail. The following passage is taken from a chapter on marketing in *Principles of Business for* CXC by Sam Seunarine ('CXC' stands for the Caribbean Examinations Council):

> Market research covers the collection and interpretation of facts that are relevant to any part of the activity of marketing. It can be divided into four main phases:

1. <u>Fundamental market research</u>. What sort of new products should the company be making? Should the company diversify into new fields, or should it concentrate on improving its existing line of business?
2. <u>Product development</u>. Once the company has decided what to produce, the results must be tested by asking groups of customers their opinion of it, before risking millions of dollars on full-scale production. This covers such things as the best size, price, colour, type of packaging.
3. <u>Distribution</u>. What are the best outlets for the product? Should it be sold direct to retailers or only to wholesalers? Should the company have its own sales force, or use agents?
4. <u>Advertising</u> or <u>media research</u>. This covers the best means of publicizing the product at the least cost. Is it best to launch the product with one big bang or spread the publicity over a longer period?

Market research consists mostly of asking people questions, although this will be backed up by gathering facts from reference books, newspapers, rival producers' catalogues, etc. (called <u>desk research</u>). A list of questions, called a <u>questionnaire</u>, is drawn up. This is skilled work; it is essential that the questions are not misunderstood, lead to a clear answer that can be recorded, and are a true test of people's reactions without putting ideas into their head. The two main means of conducting surveys are:
1. <u>By post</u>. This is simple and cheap; the main disadvantage is that a lot of people do not bother to complete and return their questionnaire.
2. <u>By personal interview</u>. Interviewers are sent out to knock on doors or stop people in the street, ask them the questions on the form and record their answers. This can be expensive. (*pp. 72–3*)

This passage illustrates the unobtrusiveness of effective textbook style. If I were reading Seunarine's book as a student, I would be left with no strong impression of the author's voice. I would, however, feel I was being told plenty about the way business works.

I have tried rewriting parts of this text and have found that it can be improved on. For example, the second half of the first sentence ('facts that are relevant to any part of the activity of marketing') is unwieldy (why not just 'facts for use in marketing'?). And the sentence beginning 'This is skilled work' should surely end with a plural ('their heads').

Most of the time, however, I found that my attempts to rewrite this passage drew my attention to its strengths. I noticed, for example, that Seunarine manages to describe the function of market research without using 'function' at all. In fact, he uses few abstract nouns – he writes very concretely. I noticed too that the text contains several very accessible colloquial phrases ('backed up by'; 'true test'; 'putting ideas in their head'; 'do not bother') without ever seeming merely chatty. And I noticed that the author is not afraid to write in short clauses or sentences ('This is skilled work'; 'This can be expensive').

The rhythm of the passage is helped by three features, namely (i) the alternation between continuous prose and numbered points, (ii) the alternation between declarative sentences and questions, and (iii) the alternation between short clauses or sentences and long ones.

Overall, for all its imperfections, this passage strikes me as a very useful model to learn from.

Conceptual clarity

I have relatively little to say on this issue, simply because it has, in effect, been dealt with in Chapters 4 and 5. There are, however, a few additional aspects we should consider.

First, there is a distinction to be drawn between (a) structuring your material carefully and (b) indicating to the reader what that structure is. To reap the full benefit of (a) it is often necessary to indulge in a little of (b). This requires sign-posting. In other words, it requires authors to include indications of the directions that their texts are going to take. Sign-posting is most common at the beginning of chapters. Authors often indicate there how a chapter relates to those that have gone before and what will be covered as the chapter unfolds.

Sign-posting is often evident also in the opening sentences of paragraphs. Let's consider, for example, the way that Robin Mayhead writes in *Understanding Literature*. I will focus on Chapter 2, 'Literature and personal experience'. In that chapter Mayhead considers the significance that various kinds of literature have for various kinds of reader. This he does by analysing passages of literature from a Nigerian novelist, Chinua Achebe, and an English poet, William Wordsworth. Here are some of Mayhead's paragraph openings:

1. 'Literature, we have said, is not about some abstract thing called "life".'
2. 'We shall start our discussion with a very simple example.'
3. 'We shall be returning to Achebe later in this chapter.'
4. 'What will our African reader make of this human experience?'
5. 'We have now to confront a further difficulty.'
6. 'What comes out of all this?'

Consider how each of these openings acts as a signpost for the reader. (1) not only provides a general theme for the chapter ahead: it also, through the past tense ('have said') indicates that this chapter will pick up on the argument of the previous one. (2) tells the reader what to expect. (3) indicates that the reader should keep Mayhead's discussion of Achebe at least in the back of his or her mind because it is not yet complete. (4) sets up a question which the forthcoming paragraph is bound to follow. In addition, by using the word 'our', the sentence makes clear that it is continuing an earlier discussion of an imagined African reader (though it also, very unfortunately, rather implies that the actual reader of Mayhead's book is not an African). (5) tells the reader both that the forthcoming paragraph will consider a 'difficulty' and, by implication through the word 'further', that the previous paragraph was also about a 'difficulty'. (6) implies that the forthcoming paragraph will offer some sort of conclusion to the discussion so far.

This is an example of brilliantly effective textbook style. Mayhead's paragraph openings not only aid readability first time round, they also help the student who is skim reading in revision to find his or her way around. In the process, Mayhead manages to convey material of considerable conceptual complexity in a way that is beautifully limpid.

A second source of conceptual difficulty is when (as we saw in Chapter 6) authors sometimes assume cultural knowledge that their readers lack. How is this to be avoided? The best method by far is for the publisher (or failing that, the author) to arrange for readers to review the manuscript. Ideally these readers will have a different background to the author's. It is no accident that the friend I asked to read my manuscript is from a younger generation, belongs to a different ethnic group, and lives on a different continent. Very often publishers forget the generational issue: do suggest using a reader significantly younger than yourself.

There are ways of sensitising yourself to those parts of the text where you are most likely to assume knowledge that your readers do not in fact possess. One is to browse through reference books, especially encyclopaedias and dictionaries of catch phrases. If you find in such books entries for references or phrases that you have used in your text, this tells you that somebody has already judged that the meaning of such terms is in need of explanation for some readers. These might well require clarification in your book.

One final point concerning conceptual difficulty: the level of difficulty can be gauged by the type of connectives used in a text. Texts that restrict themselves to such connectives as 'and', 'but', 'although' and 'because' tend to be simpler than those characterised by such connectives as 'nevertheless' and (especially) 'notwithstanding'. Connectives such as 'however' and 'moreover' come somewhere in between.

Dumbing down?

I would be surprised if no reader has been wondering whether I have been guilty of urging authors to 'dumb down'. After all, I have urged authors to avoid, or at least reduce their use of, abstract nouns, sophisticated connectives, long words, Romance vocabulary and even cultural references to such well-known figures as Robert E. Lee.

There are two ways of levelling such a charge. The first takes the form of a general lament best summarised in the question, 'Has it really come to this? Surely one has to be able to assume *some* degree of literacy on the part of their readers?'

In this form, the charge is easily dealt with. First, authors should not assume anything about their readers' attainments: as we discussed in Chapter 2, they should research them. Readers vary. Second, we should not confuse 'ought' with 'is'. Perhaps our education system *ought* to produce greater numbers of students who know full well who Robert E. Lee was: but authors have to write for readers produced by the current system, not the ideal one.

Remember too that today's students have less access to expository prose than previous generations. In school, books have been giving way to worksheets, websites and videos, and the typical language of the press and media bears little approximation to expository prose. They have less experience of such 'textbook language' as 'nevertheless' and 'consequently'.

If a textbook is not written in a language that its readers can follow, then – regardless of how elegantly, intelligently and correctly written it is – it will fail to fulfil its prime task of imparting knowledge and understanding. The publisher will be left with unsold copies.

The more sophisticated form of the charge of dumbing down is that it is precisely because today's students have so little access to expository prose and educated language that the textbook author needs to provide them with it. Whether we like it or not, the ability to use language characterised by poly-syllabic abstract nouns, Romance vocabulary and sophisticated connectives is widely taken for granted in the professions and at higher levels of education – indeed they are seen as evidence of such education. If students do not learn this language from textbooks, where will they acquire it?

I sympathise with this argument. Its great virtue is that it reminds textbook authors of their responsibility not only to impart a subject but also provide their readers with a model of educated discourse.

I have, however, been careful not to frame the arguments above in terms of absolutes (e.g. 'never use an abstract noun', 'never use "nevertheless"'). Even the Fowlers framed their principles only in terms of preferences – 'prefer the single word to the circumlocution' and so on (no guide who seriously thought we should never use long Romance words could have written 'circumlocution'!).

Textbook authors need to be aware of where the cruxes come. An author who is familiar, for example, with the claims of Saxon and Romance vocabulary can make an informed judgement about his or her own usage. Authors who lack that understanding are simply prisoners of their habits and prejudices.

Finally, one device that offers a solution to dumbing down is parallelism. By this I mean the technique of deliberately saying the something twice but in different forms. For example, a textbook author may explain a concept both in common-sense terms and in technical terms. Consider the following passage on the theory of money, taken from Chapter 6 of Heertje and Robinson, *Basic Economics*:

> Reasons for Holding Money: Firms and households use a large amount of the money they receive to meet their daily purchases of goods and services. Keynes called this wish to hold money so that it would be ready to purchase goods and services: the transactions motive. He called the money involved transactions money, but we shall call it active money. If one has active money, one can exert an effective demand for goods and services, whenever one wishes.
>
> The opposite is inactive money, kept either for emergencies (i.e. ill health) or for buying securities such as shares in firms and government stocks. These two reasons for holding money were called by Keynes respectively the precautionary and the speculative motives. Both the active and the inactive money are examples of people's preference for liquidity (i.e. for

holding funds in money and other liquid items such as three-month treasury bills). According to Keynes, the demand for active money depends mainly on the level of national income (i.e. on production of goods and services), while that for inactive money depends on the rate of interest. If production is high, demand for active money to buy goods is high. Keynes's liquidity-preference theory of interest is discussed in Chapter 12. (*pp. 90–91*)

Heertje and Robinson help the reader to understand this passage by moving between different levels of discourse. They move between plain language (e.g. 'daily purchases of goods', 'kept either for emergencies') and technical language ('the precautionary and the speculative motives'). Similarly they move between the concrete ('ill health', 'treasury bills') and the abstract ('the demand for active money depends mainly on the level of national income'). By moving between levels, the authors are able both to explain concepts and to familiarise readers with the language of economics. (It's just a shame that they mar their prose by writing 'i.e. ill health' where they should have written 'e.g. ill health'.)

Consider how they continue to move between parallel structures in their next paragraph:

> Hoarding and Dishoarding: Any transfer from active to inactive funds, made either by consumers or by producers, is called hoarding. The opposite transfer, from inactive to active funds, is called dishoarding, or the release of money. Dishoarding is exemplified by a consumer who buys a durable consumer good (e.g. a car) for the money that he has put aside in case of emergencies. He releases his money and exerts an effective demand for motor cars. In the case of hoarding, on the other hand, the effective demand is reduced, and more is put into inactive-money funds. The individual may decide to postpone purchase of a deep-freezer and hoard funds in order to purchase shares when the price of them is optimum. (*p. 91*)

Good teachers and lecturers employ this device of parallelism regularly – sometimes so naturally that they don't even know they are doing it. They use it because they can simultaneously impart subject knowledge and provide their students with a model of educated language. Good textbooks do the same.

8. Drafting and Redrafting

You may feel, after Chapter 7, that writing sounds very complicated. It might seem that there is a lot to remember. Not only does one have to get the subject matter right, but one also has to bear in mind a host of linguistic issues: pleonasm, etymology, nominalisation and so on. In fact, however, this only becomes a problem if you try to hold all of these concerns in your head at the same time. Fortunately this isn't necessary.

The reason it isn't necessary is that, when writing a manuscript, you have more than one bite at the cherry. It is quite possible – and normal and advisable – to write each part of the manuscript several times over. That is, you can draft and redraft, improving your writing in one way or another each time.

Advantages of redrafting

The main advantage of redrafting is the liberating effect that it has on the writer once he or she realises that whatever is written can always be improved later. As Howard Becker points out in *Writing for Social Scientists*, you can 'start by writing almost anything, any kind of a rough draft, no matter how crude or confused, and make something good out of it'. Becker himself enjoys this provisionality so much that he confesses to often writing 'an almost deliberately disorganized first draft'.

A second advantage of redrafting is that it allows you to focus your thinking. That is, you organise the writing process so that each stage of writing allows you to concentrate on some particular aspect of the work. The simplest example of this is when writers divide the process into two parts, namely the compositional and the secretarial. In the compositional stage, they concentrate on generating text, getting the subject matter clear (at least in their own minds) and making sure they cover the ground. In the secretarial stage they concentrate on presentation – making sure the layout is clear and appropriate, correcting the punctuation, checking the spelling and so on.

One author described the first stage as 'writing for the writer' and the second as 'writing for the reader'. In the first stage the writer is concerned simply to get material out of his or her head onto paper, without worrying about what other people would think about it (since, in fact, nobody apart from the writer would ever read it), whilst in the second stage the concern is to ensure that the material is presented in such a way that readers can get it off the page and into their heads – and make sense of it.

Most textbook authors use at least three stages in their writing, namely planning, composing and polishing. Planning usually means thinking what needs to be included and deciding how to organise it. Thinking tends to be broad brush at this stage and actual writing minimal – for each chapter, perhaps just a heading and half a dozen subheadings.

The second stage, composing, involves (as we saw above) getting the ideas into words and getting the words onto the page. In fact, that phrase 'getting the ideas into words' is a little misleading, since it implies that the writer already has the ideas and simply has to find the right words with which to clothe them. Often, however, it is the other way round: writers discover what it is they really think about a subject whilst doing the writing.

Polishing is likely to involve more than simply correcting grammar, punctuation and spelling. It also involves making the writing more concise, accurate, rhythmical, mellifluous and fluent.

Not every writer likes to break the process down so logically. Some simply try to improve their drafts each time, without concentrating on any particular aspect at any particular stage. If that works for you, you're lucky.

A further advantage of approaching writing as a process of drafting and redrafting is that it allows you to respond to other people's criticisms and suggestions. You can, for example, ask a colleague to look at a passage that you are not quite sure is accurate and, if he or she identifies any problems, you can try to overcome them at the next stage. People often prefer to be consulted at this stage, rather than when the manuscript is supposedly finished, because it gives them an opportunity to influence the book and, since they know you are expecting to rewrite it, they feel happier to point out weaknesses.

How to redraft

In order to redraft your material effectively, you need to look critically at your own work. There are three ways in which you can stimulate self-criticism. First, simply click on 'print'. It is amazing how, once your text is on paper, it will look completely different, even though the words are the same. Somehow the printed text looks more objective, almost as if it were somebody else's work. It is best always to print the text double-spaced and with wide margins so that you can begin scribbling in the gaps as soon as you can see what needs to be altered.

A second way to stimulate self-criticism is simply to sleep on it. I have frequently had the experience when writing during the evening of hitting on what I took to be a good idea only to wake the next day knowing not only that it isn't good but also why. If you are a lazy writer you will enjoy this sensation: there is nothing like allowing whoever it is that inhabits your brain at night to worry about your writing while you have a good sleep.

The third way is to put yourself in somebody else's shoes whilst reading your work. Although this could be a notional person (e.g. 'a typical fresher physics student'), it's usually better to have a particular person in mind ('what would Sam think of this?').

Once you have established a critical frame of mind, there are various approaches that you can adopt. For example, there is the top-down approach. This involves beginning to redraft by looking at the big picture: does the chapter come in the right place in the book? Have you covered all the material? Have you written too much or too little? Are the various sections of the chapter in the best order? Your thinking at this stage will be largely organisational and the changes you make large scale. For example, you might cut and paste an entire section or you might remove several hundred words altogether (though if you do, it is best to store the text in some other file, just in case you decide you need it again).

After the top-down approach it is natural to move on to the bottom-up approach. Here you begin by looking at the detail. Is that word necessary? Is the link between those two clauses clear enough? Could that long sentence be broken into two or three shorter ones?

One of the fascinations – or frustrations, depending on your state of mind – of the bottom-up approach is that a change to a single detail can have knock-on effects for other parts of the text. Removing one sentence might well require you to rewrite the sentences either side of it in order to make the links clear or the rhythm of the paragraph smoother. You might also find there are sentences later on in the chapter that assumed the existence of the sentence that is no longer there, so these too need to be rewritten or removed. Perhaps too you gave some hint, through sign-posting or through implication, of the sentence that you have now removed: those hints too have to be removed. By now you might find the whole balance of the passage subtly changing and feel that other passages need to be revised similarly. In this way you might end up revising in a dozen or more ways a chapter that had seemed finished.

I was once shown some symbols to use in redrafting that I have found useful ever since. When reading your draft, try writing the following in the margin:

↑ = expand this section; say more about this

↓ = reduce this section; be more concise or selective

⟷ = change this around

⚲ = look at this closely

It helps to have a small stock of reference books on hand to help you when you are redrafting particular sentences. I would recommend four types:

1. One of the standard general dictionaries – Oxford, Chambers, Collins, Webster's or Encarta.
2. A writers' dictionary. These are shorter and less comprehensive than general dictionaries. They concentrate on those words that commonly cause problems because writers are uncertain over their spelling, meaning or application.
3. One or two usage guides – preferably one arranged alphabetically, e.g. Eric Partridge, *Usage and Abusage* and one arranged thematically, e.g. Ernest Gowers, *The Complete Plain Words*. H. W. & F. G. Fowler, *The King's English* – is available on the internet.
4. Finally, you might consider supplementing the above with a few more specialised books such as dictionaries of confusables and troublesome words.

Useful though such resources are, the most valuable resource is the sensitivity to language that they help to develop in the writer. Indeed, it is this that helps to overcome the greatest disadvantage of reference resources, i.e. that you first have to know what it is you need to look up. Consider, for example, the fact that authors sometimes confuse 'amicable' and 'amiable'. If you know that you are confused over these words then you can easily look them up in a usage guide such as the *Bloomsbury Good Word Guide*. The problem is that you might have been merrily using one of these words to mean the other for years without ever recognising the problem – as tends to happen with confusables. If, however, you are used to looking points up regularly, or even just browsing, you will find a positive cycle develops as if by magic: the more use you make of your reference sources, the better you will be at knowing when to use them.

Case study

As an example of redrafting, let us look at how Chapter 7 of this book developed. In my book proposal, the plan for the chapter (which was originally going to be Chapter 8) said simply 'Language and style: clarity; providing a bridge between everyday and specialist jargon'. By the time I had written the complete first draft, the subtitles for the chapter ran as follows:

1. Design issues
2. Avoiding conceptual difficulties
3. Avoiding verbal difficulties
4. Avoiding syntactical and grammatical difficulties
5. Dumbing down?
6. Reference books
7. Linguistic models

The reason I had generated more subtitles was mainly because I had covered many of these issues (those of the first four sections) in the chapter on readability: having there identified various sources of difficulty in writing, I felt I now needed to say something positive about how to overcome them.

When I redrafted the chapter some weeks later, I changed the order of sections as follows:

1. Avoiding verbal difficulties (renamed 'Using words well')
2. Avoiding syntactical and grammatical difficulties (renamed 'Constructing better sentences')
3. Linguistic models (renamed 'The use of models')
4. Avoiding conceptual difficulties (renamed 'Conceptual clarity')
5. Dumbing down?

I moved the section on design issues to Chapter 9 and the section on reference books to the chapter you are reading now. This was because the first draft of Chapter 7 was too lengthy and insufficiently focused. I re-ordered the remaining sections in order to emphasise the continuity with Chapter 6 by tackling issues in the same order. I reworded the subtitles to make them less forbidding (that is, less academic and more positive).

So far, we have looked at an example of top-down redrafting. Now let us look at an example, drawn from the same chapter, of the bottom-up approach. Here is the first draft of a passage that now appears on page 94.

> Two common causes of circumlocution are euphemism (we speak of people 'passing away', 'going to meet their maker' and so on, instead of dying) and pomposity. The latter is more hazardous for textbook authors. It is easy to look at the examples that Gowers gives (for example, 'Long passages have visual unattractiveness' instead of 'Long passages look ugly') and think 'I would never write like that' and yet this kind of pomposity is very common. One cause is when the writer feels superior to his or her audience and wishes to show it, but another, more insidious, cause is when the author feels insecure – either because he or she is short of material or he or she does not have a secure grasp of the subject. The temptation is for the author to try to hide such shortcomings (certainly from the reader and perhaps even from him- or herself) adopting a pompous tone in the hope that this will give the impression of expertise.

When it came to redrafting this chapter, I found this paragraph overlong and so turned it into two shorter ones. When I came to the sentence beginning 'It is easy to look...', I found that too was overlong and so I divided it into two. I also replaced the example with a more current one which I felt was easier to appreciate without its original context than Gowers' was.

I added a sentence at the end of the passage suggesting how to overcome the problem that the paragraph had identified. I did this because Chapter 7 was supposed to be constructive, yet in the first draft of the passage I had given no advice. If you turn to page 94 you will find some other changes. You might like to speculate on why I made the changes and how, if at all, they have improved the passage.

Writers sometimes doubt the value of bottom-up redrafting. Howard Becker has given the perfect reply to such doubts. Commenting on the detailed and subtle changes that a copy-editor had made to one of his manuscripts, he wrote:

> When I read the material with her changes, I felt the way I do when, looking through the viewfinder of my camera, I give the lens that last quarter turn that brings everything into perfect focus

That captures beautifully the effect of careful bottom-up redrafting.

Redrafting: an overall view

Most writers find two things happen when they redraft a passage. First, their sentences get shorter as they either leave words out or break long sentences into two or more shorter ones. Second, they find the passage as a whole gets shorter as they eliminate padding. Some writers are reluctant to do this: they feel they worked hard to get the words out in the first place and don't want to admit that the effort was wasted. The act of tightening up your prose, however, usually feels very rewarding by the end – rather like tidying up the attic after several years and finding that much of the clobber that has collected there can go in the bin.

117

9. Presentation

Textbooks can present information verbally, symbolically (i.e. through formulae and equations) or visually (through graphs, diagrams, photographs and so on). Readers vary in their preferences concerning the way in which they like to receive information. It is best, therefore, to present information in more than one way. For example, Richard Lipsey consistently uses a variety of presentational techniques in his *Introduction to Positive Economics*. For instance, when discussing the relationship between household income and consumption (p. 20), he presents an example first in words:

> When income is zero the household will spend £800 a year (either by borrowing the money or by consuming past savings), and for every pound of income that the household obtains net of taxes... it will increase its expenditure by £0.80.

Next he presents the same relationship symbolically (using C to represent consumption and Y to represent income):

$$C = 800 + 0.8\ Y$$

Finally, he presents the relationship in the form of a graph, with consumption expenditure on the vertical axis, disposable income on the horizontal axis, and a straight line rising to the right to represent the relationship between the two.

I happen to find the symbolic relationship easiest to understand and remember. Other readers will have different preferences. For readers who respond to more than one means of presentation, the repetition of an idea in different forms provides re-enforcement. For example, when I read Lipsey's verbal presentation above, I thought I knew what he meant; when I read the symbolic presentation, I was clear that I had understood; and when I saw the graph it provided confirmation. By using all three forms, Lipsey maximises his chances of communicating with all of his readers.

Diagrams

There is little that need be said to authors (as opposed to designers) about the use of equations, formulae and graphs. And much has been said already in this book about the use of words. This chapter, therefore, concentrates on the use of diagrams.

The use of diagrams in school textbooks has improved enormously over the last decade or so. The Oxford Revision Guides even have the phrase 'through diagrams' in their titles (e.g. *Advanced Business Studies through Diagrams*). My impression of textbook publishing for college and professional courses, however, is that it is full of wasted opportunities. Haralambos, *Sociology: themes and perspectives,* for example, is rich in tables of statistics but makes little use of diagrams, whilst McLeod, *An Introduction to Counselling* relies entirely on text, despite using wide-format pages that could easily accommodate diagrams. Consider too the contrast between books on linguistics, on the one hand, and foreign language textbooks on the other. The former often make considerable use of diagrams (for example, mapping the meanings of words in semantic space). Often modern foreign language textbooks could make use of such diagrams but fail to.

As a consequence, a handful of helpful diagrams in a college or professional textbook might be sufficient to give it a competitive advantage.

There are five main types of diagram to use, namely grid, Venn, spider, tree and flow diagrams. Let us examine them one-by-one.

Grids

Grids are useful for illustrating two-dimensional models. In Chapter 5, for example, I used a grid to illustrate Cummins' curriculum model. This had two dimensions: cognitive demand and contextualisation.

This type of diagram is useful for displaying taxonomies. The grid in Chapter 5, for example, divides learning activities into four types (cognitively-undemanding/contextualised, cognitively-demanding/contextualised and so on), one per quadrant.

Grids are particularly useful when measurements on the two axes can be divided into positive and negative. For example, it can be useful in counselling and in management training to distinguish between what one person knows and what is known by the rest of the group (family, workplace, peer group etc.) of which that person is a member. Such distinctions are often illustrated diagrammatically, as in Fig. 9.1.

Known to group

		+	**-**
Known to individual	**+**	Facts known to both the individual and the group	Facts known to the individual but not the group
	-	Facts known to the group but not the individual	Facts known to neither the individual nor the group

Fig. 9.1: Grid

Venn diagrams

Venn diagrams are useful for showing the logical relationships between classes of objects or concepts. For example, suppose that a soccer team called United has a player called Smith who has scored lots of goals for them. Suppose too that they have never lost a game in which he has scored. Fig. 9.2 shows how we can represent this situation diagrammatically.

120

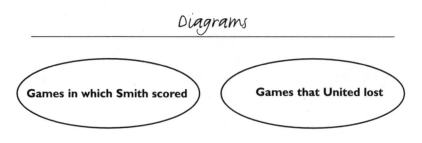

Fig. 9.2: Simple Venn diagram

Now suppose that (i) there were some games in which Smith did not score for United but somebody else did (in other words 'games in which Smith scored' is a subset of 'games in which United scored') and (ii) United lost some of these games but not all of them and (iii) there were some games in which United lost and did not score at all. Fig. 9.3 shows how we can use a Venn diagram to represent this situation.

Fig. 9.3: More complex Venn diagram

Whereas expressing such relationships in words can be cumbersome, Venn diagrams make these relationships clear at a glance.

Spiders

Spider diagrams are useful for showing how one idea has several components. For example, in geography we might be interested in explaining why a particular town developed into a popular holiday resort. Perhaps this was because (i) it had sandy beaches, (ii) an entrepreneur built a railway to it early on, (iii) the town was a spa with supposedly health-giving water and (iv) it was the nearest resort for a group of large industrial towns inland. Fig. 9.4 shows this diagrammatically.

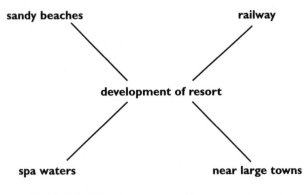

Fig. 9.4: Spider

Spider diagrams show relationships simply. For example, although the above diagram shows that the central issue had a number of factors, it does not claim to show anything about the timing or relative importance of those factors or how exactly they are related. Because of their simplicity, spiders are most useful at an early, undeveloped, stage of an argument or as an *aide-mémoire* for summing up the main points at the end of a chapter.

Trees

The best-known form of tree diagram is the family tree. Trees are useful for showing levels of hierarchy, either chronologically (as in a family tree) or logically. For instance, in textbooks on literature, a tree diagram can show the relations between various forms and genres. For example, Fig. 9.5 shows how litera-

ture is made up of three forms (prose, poetry and drama) and
how prose literature in turn comprises fiction and non-fiction:

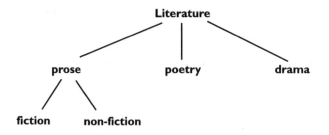

Fig. 9.5: Tree

Helmut Bonheim shows, in *Literary Systematics*, how tree and
other diagrams can be used to present a subject (i.e. literary
studies) that usually relies entirely on words.

Flow diagrams

Flow diagrams consist of arrows linking either boxes or
bubbles. Usually the arrows move either from left to right
across the page or from top to bottom. Such diagrams can be
used to illustrate the movement of ideas, information, decisions,
influence or physical objects (e.g. traffic flows). They are particularly useful for illustrating procedures, systems, processes,
algorithms or lines of causation. As a consequence, they are
popular in management books.

Various conventions can be used to make flow diagrams
more sophisticated. For example, boxes can be used to represent
objective, measurable or observable phenomena, whilst
bubbles can be used for the more subjective phenomena such
as ideas or feelings. Colour can be used to distinguish one type
of flow from another. I was once taught history by a teacher
who seemed able to represent any historical event as a flow
diagram on one side of A4 paper. He used one colour to
represent economic causes of historical change, a second colour
to represent political causes, a third to represent intellectual
causes, and so on. What a shame that he never published these
diagrams in textbook form!

Making sense through the senses

Some readers are more visually minded than others. The most obvious consequence of this is that some readers will respond more to diagrams than others. A less obvious consequence is that this might also affect the way readers respond to language.

This point has been argued by several writers in the field of management training. They point out that we vary in the way in which we employ our senses to learn about the external world. Some people – professional tasters for tea companies, for example, or restaurant critics – have a well-developed sense of taste; others, such as orchestral conductors, are acute listeners; and so on. The writers argue that we also vary in the way that we employ our senses internally, i.e. in response to language. Some people respond strongly to the language of sight: they like to talk about 'seeing a problem clearly' or 'focusing on an argument'. Others are drawn more to the language of sound: they might talk about 'tuning in' or use phrases such as 'I'm glad to hear it'. Other people might respond more to the language of taste, smell or touch: they might refer to a 'bitter' experience, for example, or of being 'touched' by an idea.

This argument, if valid, has two consequences for the authors of textbooks. It follows that, in order to reach visually minded readers, textbook authors should use both diagrams and visual vocabulary. It also follows that, in order to communicate effectively with other readers, authors should use the language of the other senses. In the course of a passage of argument or exposition, therefore, an author should try to incorporate language from each of the senses at some point.

Design issues

As part of the commissioning process, your publisher will want to arrange a meeting with you. Make sure that you discuss text design at this meeting. If your book is part of a series, it will take the series design. If it isn't, the text design will be based on other books in the publisher's list. Your publisher is unlikely to go to the expense of creating a new text design for just one book. If, however, you have noticed effective design features in competing books, do draw the editor's attention to them.

Evaluate your publisher's text design according to its appropriateness for the market rather than its aesthetic appeal. If a font conveys the wrong message about a book (for example, an old-fashioned font is being used for an avant-garde text), say so. If you just happen not to like the proposed font, tough. Remember that readers usually want a design that is familiar and unobtrusive. Novelty in text design is, therefore, usually to be avoided.

Ensure that you and your editor are clear about the number and type of figures to be included and also the number of colours to be used. It is a waste of time to design figures that depend on colour coding if your publisher has not budgeted for colour.

If your publisher has already created the text design for your book, your editor may be able to provide you with a disc with the page format already on it. John Seely, who is a hugely successful author of schools textbooks, always tries to word-process pages directly into the format the publisher intends to use. If, however, no such disc is available, there is no point fiddling around with a word processor trying to design the text yourself. Just ensure that your intentions are clear (for example, that it is clear which are the major subheadings and which are the minor).

Note that authors frequently forget to provide captions for their figures. This causes confusion and delay in the editing process.

When you have delivered the manuscript, ask to see a sample page of your text when it is first typeset, rather than waiting until the proofs are ready. You will then be able to alert your editor to any likely problems before it is too late.

When you receive proofs, do check that the typesetter has accurately distinguished between major and minor subheadings. The easiest way to ensure that the typesetter gets this right is to avoid overelaborate hierarchies of headings in the first place. Within a chapter, three levels of headings are often sufficient. Check too the chapter headings at the top of right-hand ('recto') pages. If they have been abbreviated, make sure the abbreviations are appropriate.

10. The "Extra Bits"

Let us say that you have been through all of the stages covered so far by this book. You have researched your book, found a publisher, drafted and redrafted your text, and added diagrams. You could be forgiven for feeling that you have done the important, painstaking, work and that all that remains is some minor additions – the index, for example – that can be completed quickly and easily.

You could be forgiven: but you would be wrong. What I have referred to in the title of this chapter as 'the extra bits' (not entirely accurately, as I explain later) are important. They require both time and thought.

What do I mean by 'the extra bits'? As well as the body text, your book could include any or all of the following:

- Foreword
- Acknowledgements
- Table of contents
- List of figures
- Introduction
- Questions and exercises
- Bibliography
- Notes
- Glossary
- Index(es)

Those items that precede the main text we refer to as the prelims and those that follow it are known as end matter. Let us consider the most important items one by one.

Prelims

Forewords

There is much to be said for giving your book a foreword written by somebody else. This can serve both to endorse the book and also to draw the attention of readers, especially reviewers, to what is original and valuable about it. Neither of these functions requires the foreword to be lengthy. The shorter it is, the more likely it is to be read.

The person you invite to write the foreword should be somebody in a position to write authoritatively. At the very least, he or she should have a job title that shows that they are well qualified in the field you are writing in. This indicates to the reader that whatever the writer of your foreword says about your book is worthy of attention. Preferably, the writer should have a major reputation. The more readers who have heard of your foreword writer, the more readers will think, 'Well, if so and so thinks it's a good book, it probably is'. In addition, publishers can include the name of the foreword writer on the cover of the book and on publicity material such as fliers.

Often the easiest person to approach to write your foreword is someone who works in your own organisation (for example – if you work in a college – your principal or head of school). This is better than nothing and, if you work in a prestigious organisation, it is fine. If this is not the case, then it is less than ideal: it can easily look like nepotism.

If your book has any kind of export potential, it is worth inviting someone who lives in one of the likely export territories. A publisher's rep in, say, a Chicago bookstore, will find it much easier to sell a copy of a textbook by a British author if it contains a foreword by an American.

When deciding who to invite to write a foreword, there are two types of people to avoid. Avoid controversial people, for the simple reason that many readers will distrust them. An expert who is strongly associated with the extreme right of the political spectrum, for example, would make left-wing readers wary of your book. Avoid too people whose celebrity status has nothing to do with the field your book is about: the choice of such a person would look rather desperate, as if you were unable to find anybody relevant to endorse your book.

Although forewords are generally desirable, they can be mixed blessings. It is unlikely that you will receive a foreword that is simply negative; if the person that you have approached really doesn't like your book, he or she will simply ask to be excused from writing for you. Sometimes, however, the foreword laces some generally positive comments with a few reservations. The question is then what to do about it. One approach is for your publisher to enquire politely whether the writer might be prepared to revise the text a little. Another is for the publisher to decide not to use the foreword at all.

An interesting example is the foreword by Reg Revans to Ortrun Zuber-Skerritt, *Action Research in Higher Education*. Revans actually devotes more words to characterising his own work than to Zuber-Skerritt's and focuses more on the question of which of the two writer's work is better (rather than on the qualities of the book itself). Although the foreword feels somewhat ungenerous as a result, it benefits the book because Revans' reputation in the field is considerable. To be able to present the book 'with a foreword by Reg Revans' (which, incidentally, the publisher failed to do, at least on the cover) gives the book status.

Acknowledgements

There are three reasons for acknowledging someone: for legal reasons; politeness or gratitude; and as a marketing device.

Most publishers who give permission to quote copyright material in your book will stipulate that it is conditional on acknowledgement in the book.

People who have put themselves out for you obviously deserve acknowledgement. The difficulty is to know where to draw the line. Remember that the longer the list of acknowledgements is, the less likely it is that anyone will read them, so be careful not to devalue your offers of thanks by including too many. There is no need, for example, to thank librarians who have done for you no more than their job normally entails. If, on the other hand, they have shown unusual enthusiasm, initiative or diligence, then they deserve thanks.

An acknowledgement can act as a marketing device by associating your book with a well-known name. If, for example, you have had help from an internationally acknowledged expert on a particular topic, then some of their lustre might attach itself to your book if you mention them. Don't abuse this, however, by listing people who are unfamiliar with the project or who are less than enthusiastic about your work. Provided you don't abuse the device, you will find that people rather like seeing their name in print and will find reasons for drawing other people's attention (especially their students') to the book. That I have mentioned Gordon Pradl's *Literature for Democracy* to several people (oops, I've just done it again) is not entirely unrelated to the fact that my name appears in the acknowledgements. I don't think I am unusually vain in this matter!

Introductions

Introductions have two main functions. One is sign-posting – indicating to the reader what the book is going to cover and what approach it will take. The other is setting the context for the rest of the book. The need for either function is questionable. Often there are sufficient signposts for the reader – the book's title and subtitle, the table of contents, the opening paragraphs of each chapter and so on – and so additional sign-posting in the introduction is redundant. The provision of a context is, in contrast, often useful. If, however, the discussion is of any length, it is best to take it out of the introduction and entitle it 'Chapter 1'. After all, many readers skip introductions.

You do not necessarily need an introduction at all. Often it is best just to dive in and get the book moving.

Questions and exercises

The central theme of this chapter is that parts of your book that might be considered marginal are in fact integral. Of no item is this more true than questions and exercises for student readers. In some areas of textbook publishing this is perfectly obvious. Indeed, in some areas of schools publishing, an author might write nothing but questions. For example, the books written by James Driver for the *Comprehension Success* series published by Oxford University Press (OUP) consist entirely of pages from other books printed on the left-hand pages and questions by the author on the right-hand pages. The reason I have left the business of questions and answers until now, rather than discuss them in Chapter 7, is simply that in textbooks in other areas of publishing they play a less central, and indeed perhaps optional, role.

The most important point about questions is to be clear what the point of them is. You might include questions to:

- Encourage readers to look back and re-read key parts of the text
- Enable readers to check their comprehension
- Enable teachers to check their students' comprehension
- Make life easier for teachers by providing assignments for class work, homework or course work
- Provide students with experience of examination-style questions
- Develop readers' understanding further
- Enable readers to apply their understanding to new situations

Be clear too about how your questions relate to the syllabus and assessment criteria of the courses that your textbook covers. If, for example, the syllabus lists some key skills, it is desirable for you to include a set of questions aimed at each of these skills. For example, OUP's *Comprehension Success* provides three sets of questions on each page. The first set tests recall; the second tests inferential reading; and the third tests the ability to apply information creatively. It is no mere accident that these three skills form a central and explicit part of the National Curriculum for England and Wales, i.e. the curriculum that most of the book's readers follow.

I find that, when setting questions, textbook authors are often drawn to some interrogatives at the expense of others. For example, an author might draft numerous questions beginning 'what' or 'which' and forget to pose any beginning with 'how'. Review the questions you have drafted to see whether you have used the whole range of interrogatives ('what', 'when', 'where', 'which', 'why', 'who' and 'how'). Using the whole range tends to provide variety and to broaden the range of skills that you are testing. In particular, 'how' and 'why' questions tend to test high-level comprehension skills rather than just recall.

For some reason writers often confuse the meanings of 'how' and 'why' questions. Many questions beginning 'why' cause readers problems simply because they are really 'how' questions in disguise. I don't know why this should be. If in doubt, try substituting the following phrases for the interrogative: 'in what way?'; 'on what ground?'; 'for what reason?'; and 'with what purpose?'. If the first phrase is the best substitute, use 'how'; if one of the others, use 'why'.

It is usually desirable to step your questions, i.e. to begin with the easiest questions and to end with the hardest. The advantage of this is that it develops readers' confidence: they begin each set of questions with ones that they are likely to be able to answer. Stepping is also extremely useful for teachers by helping them to differentiate the work that they set. Able students, for example, can be told to leave out the early questions and go straight to the harder ones at the end. We have already seen in Chapter 5 how, using Jim Cummins' model, questions can be stepped according to the cognitive demands involved in a task *and* the degree of contextualisation provided.

Think back too to the discussion in Chapter 4 of Kolb's theory of learning styles. By setting questions aimed at each of the four styles of learning identified there you are likely to appeal to, and develop, all of your readers.

A key distinction to bear in mind is that between closed and open questions. Closed questions are those for which only a limited number of (usually short) answers are available. Open questions allow more diverse, less predictable and, perhaps, lengthy answers. Questions beginning 'do you agree...' are closed: they are likely to be answered simply 'yes' or 'no' (or possibly 'don't know'). Questions beginning 'how far do you agree?' or 'what reasons for agreeing or disagreeing can you find?' are much more open. Closed questions are useful for checking comprehension. Open questions are useful for stimulating discussion, argument, extended writing and more advanced thinking.

Take, for example, the kind of questions that feature in *Good Practice in Child Care* by Janet Kay. The book includes numerous boxes containing descriptions of situations followed by questions for thought and discussion. Here is an example from the first draft:

Think of an aspect of your role or work in your placement or work setting – for example, a work practice or routine, the way in which the setting is laid out, the resources and how they are used, the priorities of staff and management. Having chosen an aspect, consider... the following questions:

1. Does it contribute to good standards in childcare?
2. To what extent are the needs of the children best met in this way?
3. Could it be done differently?

Question (2) is an open question that is likely to prompt reflection and debate. Questions (1) and (3), however, are closed questions which might elicit nothing more than a 'yes' or 'no' from the reader. In the second draft, Janet changed the first question to 'How far does it contribute...?' and the third question to 'How could it be done differently?'. The addition of 'how' and 'how far' made the questions more appropriate by converting them into open questions.

Another way of providing variety in your questions is to ensure that, where possible, you cover the following in each set of questions:

- both comparisons and contrasts, similarities and differences
- the past, present and future
- people, objects and activities or processes
- the big picture and the detail

Usually it is clear where in the book your questions or exercises should appear. The most obvious place is at the end of each chapter. Occasionally, there is an argument for placing them elsewhere. Take, for example, *Key Issues in Education and Teaching* by John Wilson. This book consists of a series of philosophical essays. It was designed primarily as a textbook for students in initial teacher training. However, because Wilson is a philosopher with a long-established, international, reputation and the essays are lucidly and entertainingly written, I felt that there might be a wider market for the book; educational philosophers and some in-service teachers might be interested in the book. Such purchasers would, however, be put off if the book looked as though it was intended solely as a student textbook. I therefore moved Wilson's questions from the end of each chapter to a section at the back of the book. My thinking was that individual purchasers flicking through the book in a shop would see that, although the book could be used as a textbook, it was also designed for a more general readership.

A contrasting example is provided by Rob Pope in *The English Studies Book*. As we saw in Chapter 5, Pope intended the book to work like hypertext (with much jumping to and fro between sections) rather than sequentially. Rather than place questions at the end of chapters, therefore, he placed them immediately after each subsection.

End matter

References

There are various ways of setting out references. When a publisher offers you a contract, he or she will provide you with notes specifying which style is required. Do oblige. Any variance will cause unnecessary delay and expense.

If you are writing a sample chapter that might end up being sent to several publishers, I strongly recommend that you use referencing software such as EndNote™. With such software, you enter into a database the details of the books and articles you are citing. Once you have done that, the software will, at the click of a mouse, convert your references to whatever style you require. This enables you to send your sample chapter in whichever style the particular publishing house requires.

When you are making notes, or copying a quotation, from a book, record the Dewey number (or other library reference number) and ISBN. This saves time if you ever need to obtain the book again. If you are copying a quotation that runs over from one page of your source to another, indicate in your notes with an oblique where the page break comes. Then, if you decide to use only part of the quotation, you can be sure which page(s) that part appeared on. You can then give the reference without going back to the source.

Glossary

We saw in Chapter 5 that Richard Lipsey urged readers of his *Introduction to Positive Economics* to 'make [their] own glossary of technical terms, committing the definitions to memory'. I questioned why readers should have to do this when Lipsey could have provided his own glossary. Of course, Lipsey's readers might well not go to these lengths: they might instead look up a term in the index and then refer to the pages where a term is first explained. This, however, is fiddly. In contrast, a glossary can be book-marked by the reader for easy reference.

That is the main advantage of a glossary. A second advantage is that it can help to make a book accessible to readers from export territories. For example, a British textbook on education is likely to refer to institutions such as Ofsted. 'Ofsted' might mean nothing to readers abroad. The author could include a parenthetical statement, explaining that Ofsted is a publicly funded organisation for inspecting schools (its name derived from the phrase Office for Standards on Education). But such an explanation, which is in any case unnecessary for British readers, obstructs the movement of the text. If there is a glossary to which the reader can refer for the explanation, the problem is solved.

The disadvantage of glossaries is that the definitions within them tend to be brief. As a result, there is a danger of being reductive.

Index

An index has three functions: to show the location of an item; to indicate the coverage of a book; and to guide the reader. If an index simply fulfilled the first two functions it would, in effect, be nothing more than a more detailed version of the contents page arranged alphabetically. It is the final function that makes an index something more than that.

An index guides the reader by re-enforcing the conception of the subject presented by the book as a whole. It can do this principally through the choice of cross- (i.e. 'see also') references. Imagine, for example, two textbooks on education, each with a chapter on assessment. One might treat this subject in isolation, in which case the cross-references from index items for this chapter (marking, testing, report-writing and so on) are likely to refer the reader only to other items within the chapter. The other book might see the business of assessment as intricately inter-related to its context. In this case, the cross-references are likely to take the reader beyond the chapter into other areas such as curriculum and pedagogy.

Authors are often surprised to discover that indexing is usually their responsibility. Indeed, this sometimes causes moral outrage, based on the belief the publisher is exploiting the author by demanding something that publishers should provide for themselves. In fact, indexes are like anything else: they require work and therefore represent an expense. Most publishers will willingly contract somebody other than the author to compile an index – but they will expect to pay such an author less in terms of royalty than authors who provide the index themselves. You should certainly ensure that you are clear what your contract says about the responsibility for compiling, or paying for the compilation of, your index. Note, however, that because the index provides a means of guiding your reader and underlining your conception of the subject, there is much to be said for compiling the index yourself.

The question then is how to approach the task. From the outside, the business of compiling an index sounds very straightforward. Surely you just decide which items you want to index, use the search function on your word processor to locate the words in the text, and then place them in alphabetical order?

Deciding which items to index

Compiling an index requires both time and thought. Each of the above steps is more complex than it first appears and each requires judgement. First, consider the question of which items to include in the index. To decide this intelligently you will have to decide the degree of exhaustivity and the degree of specificity of your index.

Exhaustivity refers to the extent to which an index makes items retrievable. At the lowest level of exhaustivity, the contents of a book are summarised by a few terms. At the highest level, every particular (person, event, object etc.) is mentioned. Highly exhaustive indexes have the advantage of completeness, but can be excessively long and cumbersome. Indexers usually have to settle for a level of exhaustivity somewhere between the two extremes.

Consider the case of *How Exams Really Work* by J. G. Lloyd (not in fact a textbook, but the example is nonetheless relevant). For this book the indexer (who was the author) opted for a low degree of exhaustivity. As editor I was happy with this because of the way the index related with the table of contents. The latter broke the text (which was only 50 000 words long) into eight chapters and listed several subheadings under each chapter heading. I decided that the combination of the two devices made it easy for readers to find what they needed.

Specificity is closely related to exhaustivity. It refers to the level in conceptual hierarchy at which an item is indexed. Consider the following hierarchy, for example:

In a textbook on art, the indexer has to decide which levels are too detailed or too general to be included. In the example of

How Exams Really Work, the index complemented the table of contents by concentrating on more specific items. One of the headings in the table of contents, for example, was 'The examiners' (which is fairly general). The index excluded this term but included more specific terms such as 'Chief examiners' and 'Principal examiners'.

Searching for index items

Now consider what is involved in searching for items in the text. Many authors assume that, once they have decided which items to index, the search function on their word processor will do the rest. (This of course assumes that the publisher has provided a disc with the proofs. If not, it is a waste of time searching the original manuscript on disc, since both the text and pagination will have changed.) In fact, the search function is of little use. It will fail to:

- recognise synonyms ('whisky' and 'scotch')
- distinguish between homonyms (e.g. 'field' in the sense of a patch of grass and 'field' in the sense of an area of enquiry or research)
- identify cognates (e.g. 'run', 'runner', 'running' and 'ran')

There is no substitute for reading the proofs through from cover to cover.

Arranging items in alphabetical order

This might sound a straightforward task for any literate person. It is in fact a little more complex. First, you need to decide which form of alphabetical order to follow: word-by-word or letter-by-letter. Consider an index containing the following items: 'South Australia'; 'South Carolina'; 'Southampton'; and 'Southborough'. The word-by-word method produces the following sequence:

South Australia
South Carolina
Southampton
Southborough

Arrangement letter-by-letter (i.e. ignoring breaks between words) produces the following:

> Southampton
> South Australia
> Southborough
> South Carolina

In addition, there is the difficulty of compound headings. This is most obvious with people's names. 'Alain Robbe-Grillet' should obviously be indexed as 'Robbe-Grillet, Alain': the hyphen makes it clear how to treat the surname. But what about the novelist Harriet Beecher Stowe, whose maiden name was Beecher? Whichever name you index her under (I would file her under B for 'Beecher Stowe', because that it how most students of literature would hear her referred to), there should be a cross-reference (e.g. 'Stowe – see Beecher Stowe').

The index overall

Each of the above processes – deciding which items to index, locating the items and arranging them alphabetically – requires the indexer to make judgements. The solution is always to consider:

- the requirements of the publisher
- the needs of the book's users

Publishers will usually set a limit to the length of the index and this will constrain your decisions over the level of exhaustivity and specificity. They will also usually have a house style that will determine such issues as whether to use letter-by-letter or word-by-word arrangement.

When considering the needs of your users, bear in mind that there will probably be more than one type of user. In most cases it is helpful to consider the following types:

- the teachers or lecturers using your book to support their courses
- students following a course (especially individual learners)
- students revising at the end of a course

When you think that you have finalised your index, treat what you have as a first draft and edit it. Ensure that, whatever decisions you have made, you have applied them consistently. And, above all, avoid the notorious trap of cross-references of the following, circular, kind:

> A – see B
> B – see C
> C – see A

Conclusion

Many authors find writing 'the extra bits' rather tiresome. Usually this is not so much because of the time and thought required, but rather because the time and thought is greater than they imagined. I hope that this chapter will eliminate this frustration by helping you to anticipate. Do remember that, if done well, 'the extra bits' can give your book an advantage over its competitors.

Part Three: Taking it Further

11. Keeping Your Book in Print

Once your book has been published, you will want to keep it in print. There are two ways in which you can do this. You can help your publisher to market the book – good marketing leads to high sales, which makes the book more profitable for the publisher to reprint, which prolongs the life of the book – and you can work with the publisher to prepare new editions.

Marketing

Some authors are surprised to find that they have a role in marketing: they assume that marketing is the publisher's job. Some even object to working on marketing at all. I once gave a talk at the Society of Authors that included a passage about the ways in which authors could contribute to the marketing of their books. One of the authors there said that he didn't think he *should* help: that was his publisher's job.

I was rather taken aback by this response and I still don't understand the thinking behind it. So far as I am concerned, both the publisher and the author have a vested interest in ensuring that a book sells well: the more it sells, the more revenue the publisher receives and the more the author earns through royalties. Once the author and the publisher have agreed a royalty rate, they are, therefore, on the same side. There are enough opponents in the market place – competition in textbook publishing is tough – without the publisher and the author taking sides against each other.

Marketing, after all, is not a zero-sum game: there is no need to assume that the more an author does to promote his or her book, the less the publisher will do. In my experience it is usually the other way round: marketing departments respond to enthusiastic authors by increasing their own efforts, partly because enthusiasm is infectious and partly because publishers get excited about those books that are starting to move.

Of course, it may be that my questioner had a publisher whose marketing was just inadequate, so that he really did have to do all the work. If that was the case, however, the conclusion to draw is simply that he signed up with the wrong publisher and shouldn't make the same mistake next time. Meanwhile, lack of co-operation on his part is not going to make an inadequate publisher into an adequate one.

Your contribution to marketing will begin before the book is published and perhaps even before you have finished writing the manuscript. Your first contribution is likely to be completing an author questionnaire. This will ask you questions such as the following:

- Which publications and websites should review copies be sent to?
- Which influential people should receive complimentary copies?
- Who should fliers be sent to?
- Which conferences or exhibitions should the book be displayed, sold or promoted at?
- Which organisations or networks might be useful in helping to promote your book?
- What scope is there for press or media coverage?
- Who could be approached to endorse the book?

You will, of course, have done much of the homework for these questions when you prepared your book proposal.

Devote some thought to the questionnaire. In particular, remember the distinction between trade publishing and academic or professional publishing. It does no harm to suggest to your publisher that copies of your book be sent to prestigious national newspapers or glossy international magazines, but remember to give chapter and verse on the channels that count for most in textbook publishing – academic journals, newsletters and websites run by professional associations, and so on. Some books that I have commissioned have received plenty of national news coverage without much benefit to sales. Good reviews, on the other hand, often produce noticeable increases in sales.

When suggesting names of people to receive complimentary copies, by all means indulge a daydream or two about representatives of the great and the good receiving your book ecstatically, but give more attention to people who are well placed to influence sales directly, e.g. course leaders, heads of department and lecturers with multitudes of students.

Remember the scope for coverage in the local press and on local radio. Often these media are more hard-pressed for material. It is unlikely that the publication of a textbook will be thought newsworthy in its own right, but if your book covers topical issues then it might lead to invitations to write articles or give interviews on those topics. Be sure, however, not to leave the newspaper or programme editor with the job of spotting that the book covers such issues: point it out in the covering letter. If the local newspaper does carry an article by or about you, insist endlessly that the article mentions the title and publisher (and, ideally, the price and ISBN) of your book. Similarly, if you appear on local radio, say beforehand that you would like the presenter to mention your book's title and publisher and, if it looks as though he or she has forgotten, slip it in yourself. There is no need to be embarrassed about this: the media are used to people using them to publicise products and depend on this for copy.

It is useful for a book to carry endorsements, either on its cover or on promotional material. This is particularly important if you are not yet well known. If your book has export potential, suggest that your publisher approaches people in the most likely export territories for some of the endorsements.

The authors who help to market their books most successfully tend to think ahead, assert themselves and be persistent. If, for example, there is a conference to be held in six months' time and you think your publisher might not be aware of it, let them know in good time. They need to prepare a conference schedule, allocate a conference budget and dispatch books from their warehouse. If you leave it until the day before to phone up, prepare to be disappointed.

Keep liaising with your publisher after publication. If, for example, a newsletter (published, say, by a subject association or trade union) is producing a special edition that is ideally suited to your book, the fact that it might be a year since the book was published should not prevent you checking that the marketing department knows about it.

There is a difference between being assertive and being aggressive. I commissioned one author who complained endlessly about the failure of his previous publisher's marketing department. Shortly after publication I was bombarded with angry phone calls, faxes and e-mails demanding to know why I had failed to send out complimentary copies to people on the list that he had sent me. The problem was that I had never received the list. When I did receive it, I ensured that the copies were dispatched efficiently – and then vowed never to lift a finger to help the author if I didn't have to. That might not have been the most rational response on my part, but I guess most editors would do the same. Nobody objects to authors ensuring that their books are taken seriously and handled professionally – indeed, one rather respects it – but that can be done, and is best done, without aggression.

How much you can contribute to the marketing of your book will depend on how familiar your publisher is with the field. If they have already published several books in your subject area and/or at the same level as your book, they will know all about the main channels already and have plenty of ideas of their own. In this case you might have little to contribute. It is difficult to believe, however, that there is ever a case where the author has nothing at all to offer. You will probably know more about your local scene, however familiar your publisher is with national marketing channels.

New editions

If your book sells well, it is likely that, sooner or later, the question of a new edition will arise. What triggers a new edition? How welcome is a new edition likely to be? And how should you go about working on it?

Triggers

There are a number of developments that can trigger a new edition. The most obvious is a change in either the curriculum that your book is designed to support or the way in which the curriculum is assessed. In schools publishing this is usually the only trigger.

If the changes in curriculum or assessment are major, your book will simply die without a new edition. If the changes are minor, the book might survive without a new edition – teachers and lecturers are reluctant to change from books that they know and trust – but it will be less attractive, particularly to newly trained staff who have yet to develop any loyalty to your product. Because even minor changes will make your book less competitive, even they are likely to trigger a new edition.

A second trigger for a new edition might be a change in the context in which your book is used. For example, in the UK students in initial teacher training used to study textbooks about education mostly whilst they were in college; now they complete more assignments whilst working in schools on teaching practice. Consequently the textbooks they use now need to stand alone, without the support of college tutorials. The books can also now include material designed to inter-relate with the students' own teaching experience.

Another possible trigger consists of changes in subject matter. New research is published; perspectives change; some topics grow in importance, others wither. When, for example, Asa Briggs wrote the second edition of *The Age of Improvement*, his textbook on the history of Victorian Britain (first published 1959; second edition 2000), he cited 'the many developments in historical scholarship' as the main trigger.

Finally, a new edition might be triggered by the perception that changes are necessary in order to satisfy a particular export territory. For example, after publishing *Economics* by the American economist Joseph E. Stiglitz, W.W. Norton decided that the book would do better in the UK if there were a new edition prepared by a British author (in this case, John Driffill).

How welcome is a new edition?

Publishers have mixed views on new editions. The main disadvantages are the costs of developing a new edition (editing, typesetting and marketing), the fact that unsold copies of the old edition will prove unsaleable and will have to be remaindered or pulped, and the fact that changes might cause lecturers or teachers who have used the book so far to reconsider their choice.

On the other hand, through updates and improvements the new edition becomes more competitive. It also provides an opportunity to sell the book all over again. This attracts publishers because it carries less risk than publishing an entirely new book. Some customers (especially libraries) who bought the first edition will buy the second too and there is the chance to attract new customers. If the book is well established, the publisher might also see an opportunity to increase the price.

Acquisitions editors sometimes have their own reasons for proposing a new edition. An editor struggling to reach an annual target for the number of new books signed might just see the commissioning of new editions as the easiest solution.

Overall, provided that the triggers have been foreseen (so that excessive stock of the first edition is not left in the warehouse), publishers will welcome the opportunity of a new edition as a way of capitalising on existing intellectual property.

Authors also have mixed views over new editions. Be in no doubt that a new edition is likely to involve plenty of work. 'I did not understand at first how much work would be involved and how long various stages in the process might take' was John Driffill's comment on having completed the British edition of *Economics*. That is a common experience. Authors often find that the various parts of their book are more inter-related than they realised. The consequence is that changes in one part of the book entail (unforeseen) changes elsewhere.

On the other hand, a new edition will involve far less work than the writing of the first edition and provide increased returns on that initial endeavour. Overall, therefore, authors tend to welcome the proposal of a new edition unless their circumstances have changed in the meantime.

Preparing a new edition

A new edition will involve a rerun of some of the research entailed in writing the first edition (as outlined in Chapter 2). At the very least you will want to ensure that you understand what triggered the new edition and what implications that has. In addition, you have the opportunity to research responses to the first edition. Such responses vary from the formal (reviews in journals) to the informal. Asa Briggs looked at what users of the first edition of *The Age of Improvement* had scribbled in the margins ('"rubbish" is the most eloquent [comment], but ticks and crosses also matter'). Somewhere in between, and of most value, come interviews with users of the first edition – time invested in these will repay itself.

There are three questions that you need to consider. First, can you do it yourself? If your circumstances have altered and you are no longer able to work on the book, explore the possibility of using a co-author. This is a classic method for keeping a book in print when the author has retired. If the trigger is the need for an export edition, you will in any case need a co-author from the export territory unless you have worked there recently yourself.

The second question is whether the length should change. Editions often grow in length as authors add new material without removing any of the original. This makes the book more comprehensive. However, it also increases production costs. If the market is sensitive to changes in price, your publishers will resist this because the increase in costs will squeeze profit margins. If, on the other hand, the market is more flexible, then a longer book can carry a higher price and actually increase margins. A number of textbooks in my own lists (e.g. *Teaching in Further Education* by L. B. Curzon) have increa-sed in extent with happy results for all concerned. Ensure that you discuss the question of extent carefully with your editor before embarking on a new edition.

The third question is whether to work within the existing structure of the book, adding a little here and perhaps trim-ming a little there, or to make wholesale changes. The problem with the latter is not simply that it involves more work but also that it disconcerts teachers and lecturers who have built your book into the delivery of their courses. Just as most home-owners tend to make alterations and build extensions, rather than knock down a house and start again, it is best to avoid wholesale changes if possible.

A case study

Let's look in detail at one example of a new edition of a textbook. Andrew Pollard's *Reflective Teaching in the Primary School* is a highly successful textbook written for students in initial teacher training (ITT). When I started work on the book it was already in its third edition. We decided to embark on a new edition because the business of primary (i.e. elementary) schooling was changing rapidly, mainly in responses to changes in educational policy and legislation. Sales figures had held up well, suggesting that the book had not become seriously dated. However, we decided to act before the risk of declining sales set in: it is much easier to retain market share than regain it – and, in any case, we wanted to increase it.

Andrew's research for the new edition provides a model of how to proceed. First, he obtained current and projected figures for the number of ITT students in each college. We matched these up against our sales data so that we could see which the key customers were: we wanted to ensure that colleges already adopting the book continued to do so and we wanted to encourage other colleges as potential adopters. Fortunately, Andrew had a number of contacts at these colleges whom he could consult in order to find out what they would require from, and welcome in, a textbook. This he did partly by postal survey and partly by face-to-face contact. These consultations produced a number of valuable responses that made it much easier for us to provide what our existing and potential customers most wanted.

As the editor for the project I decided that we should retain the text design and elements of the cover design for the book. My reasoning was:

1. The text design was already suitable. The pages were large enough (244 mm by 169 mm) to carry diagrams and boxed material and carried enough words per page (approximately 600) to prevent a lengthy text becoming too fat.

2. Continuity in at least some elements of the cover design was desirable because, although I didn't like the design, the elements that we retained would symbolise to lecturers who had adopted the book that the new edition would not be radically different.

Further continuity was provided by the decision to support the book with a web page cross-referencing the index of the new edition to that of the previous edition. We did this because I had noticed that lecturers sometimes complained when we published new editions because the page numbers in their course notes had to be updated.

Conclusion

If you have gone to the considerable trouble of writing a textbook you will want to make the most of it when it is published. Collaborating with your publisher on the marketing of the book and the production of new editions are the most effective ways of doing this. Some authors find the labour involved less creative than the writing of the original manuscript, others find it as creative but in a different way: but in terms of returns for labour expended, both activities are highly efficient.

12. Textbooks in the Electronic Age

What is the future of the textbook in the electronic age? What are the implications of digitalisation for authors of textbooks? The answers vary according to the medium under consideration.

Take CD-ROMs, for example. They have made a considerable impact on reference publishing. One public librarian recently told me that he spent his entire reference budget on CD-ROMs. They are well suited to the demands of reference reading, in which the reader often reads only small units of text and frequently moves from one unit to another in order to follow up cross-references. Moreover, it is cheaper for publishers to update CD-ROMs than to keep printing new editions of books on paper. However, they have had much less impact on textbook publishing. In part this is because textbooks involve more sustained reading of continuous passages, at least at college and professional level. It is also because textbooks need updating less frequently. And, finally, it is because CD-ROMs are unwieldy, requiring hardware that is expensive and stationary. For similar reasons, interactive video has had virtually no impact on textbook publishing. CD-ROMs remain popular in primary (elementary) schools when publishers produce them as supplements to textbook series, but this is likely to change as that sector becomes more familiar with the internet as an alternative medium. For all of these reasons, this chapter will concentrate instead on the current and future impact of the internet.

Death of the textbook?

Will digitalisation lead to the death of the textbook? It is not difficult to see why many people say that it will. As Samuel Cameron argued in the *THES*:

why should a student shell out the near £30.00 required in this age of copious handouts and cheaply available internet material? For example, David Friedman's complete text *Price Theory: an intermediate Text* is on the internet at zero cost.

In fact, David Friedman's website provides the reader with more than his publisher ever did. *Price Theory* was previously published in printed form and went to a second edition. On his website Friedman provides not only the complete text of the second edition but also two chapters from the first edition that were omitted from the second. Printing and paper costs put pressure on publishers to exclude material: there is no equivalent cost on the internet.

A second reason why many people believe that digitalisation will destroy textbook publishing is the possible impact of micropayments. With a printed book, the consumer has either to buy the whole book or none of it: he or she cannot buy only the part that interests them. This constitutes an important disadvantage of textbook publishing. Research by the Council of Academic and Professional Publishers found that 31% of students find less than half of the textbook material they purchase useful. Micropayments on the internet should enable readers to select and pay for only those passages that they want to read. This makes electronic text much more flexible than the printed version.

A third reason why digitalisation might be seen as lethal for textbook publishing is the impact it might have on reading habits. In *The Gutenberg Elegies*, Sven Birketts has drawn attention to the difference between reading printed and electronic media. Print:

> posits a time axis; the turning of pages, not to mention the vertical descent down the page, is a forward-moving succession, with earlier contents at every point serving as a ground for what follows. Moreover, the printed material is static – it is the reader, not the book, that moves forward...

> Materials are layered; they lend themselves to re-
> reading and to sustained attention. The pace of
> reading is variable, with progress determined by the
> reader's focus and comprehension. (*p. 122*)

Electronic text, according to Birketts, is very different:

> Contents, unless they are printed out...are felt to be
> evanescent. They can be changed or deleted with the
> stroke of a key. With visual media...impression and
> linear sequentiality are sacrificed. The pace is rapid,
> driven by jump-cut increments, and the basic move-
> ment is laterally associative rather than vertically
> cumulative. (*p. 122*)

Birketts is clear that the shift from printed word to electronic
text is changing our reading habits. In fact, he goes much
further. Because he believes that the reading of print is a much
more interior act than the reading of electronic text, he argues
that displacement of the former by the latter is changing our
very selves by destroying our interiority. As a consequence,
electronic text will, according to Birketts, destroy our ability to
read traditional printed books. Indeed, it will destroy our
ability even to write them:

> The complexity and distinctiveness of spoken and
> written expression, which are deeply bound to trad-
> itions of print literacy, will gradually be replaced by a
> more telegraphic sort of 'plainspeak.' (*p. 128*)

Survival of the textbook?

On the other hand, many people in the publishing industry
argue that the textbook will continue to live healthily, at least
for the foreseeable future. They point to a number of deficiencies in electronic text.

First, there is the inadequacy of the technology itself. The
most obvious example is screen technology. Most of us are
happy to use the internet to look up sports results, check share

prices and so on, but who ever settles down to reading the equivalent of a few hundred pages of a book on screen? Manufacturers of e-books are experimenting with ways of making electronic text more readable (using electronic ink, for example), but they have yet to match the readability of conventional ink printed onto paper.

The inadequacy of the technology is not just a matter of readability. It also involves what Birketts calls the 'ungainliness':

> Not only is the user affronted aesthetically at every moment by ugly type fonts and crude display options, but he has to wheel and click the cumbersome mouse to keep the interaction going. This user, at least, has not been able to get past the feeling of being infantilized. No matter how serious the transaction taking place, I feel as though my reflexes are being tested in a video arcade. I have been assured that this will pass, but it hasn't yet. (*p. 162*)

In addition, students using information technology frequently lack the knowledge needed to take anything like full advantage of the technology available. Colleges and schools often spend more money on their hardware and software than they do on training users how to use them. Next time you are using a word processor, explore the menu bar. How many of the options offered by the various drop-down menus do you use?

There is also the problem of how to charge for electronic text. So far, publishers have relied on subscription charges. Typically, these have enabled users to access very large amounts of text for specified periods of time. The charges have been correspondingly large. This has deterred individuals from subscribing, especially since any one user might want access to only a small part of the material covered by the subscription. As a result it has been mainly libraries and businesses that have paid subscriptions.

Jakob Nielsen and others have proposed the use of micropayments as a solution. Micropayments enable readers to access small amounts of information by making small payments. The payments are made at the time of downloading, unlike subscriptions which are payable in advance. Nielsen acknowledges that micropayments requiring a dollar or more per page have been unpopular with consumers but, in response to the view that internet users do not like being 'nickeled and dimed' he argues that 'the problem is being dimed; not being nickeled':

> On the Web, users should not worry about a cent per page. <u>If a page is not worth a cent, then you should not download it in the first place.</u> Even as the web grows in importance in the future, most people will probably access less than 100 non-free pages per day... Most users will have $10–$30 in monthly service charges for Web content.

The problem here is that Nielsen deals only with demand for on-line content: he ignores the question of whether such pricing would make on-line publishing profitable for the supplier. Here we need to remember that, although on-line publishing incurs no cost for paper and printing (or rather, to the extent that the user prints the material, it transfers the cost directly to the consumer), publishers still incur editorial, marketing and design costs.

Even if the problem with the economics of micropayments is resolved, there remains a problem. Although it sounds very attractive to students to be able to pay for only those parts of a textbook relevant to the assignments they're working on at any one time, in practice it would mean that they were always reading passages out of context. For example, an economics student working on, say, the function of money could pay for passages on that topic (and no other) from, say, a dozen textbooks. That student would, however, have to guess what comes before and after the passage from each book. He or she would be able to see that the treatment of the topic varied from book to book but, because the student would have no idea of the overall approach of each book, would not know why it varied. Using micropayments in this way would result in the student having more pages and less context and thus more information but less understanding.

A further problem for on-line publishing is the need for branding. Simply posting material on the internet will not ensure that it gets used. Readers will want to be sure that the material is of a high quality from a reputable and reliable source. To achieve this, on-line publishers need, like their paper-based counterparts, to invest in building a brand. The costs incurred, which are considerable, add to the expense of the product.

Some case studies

There are, then, arguments for and against the view that digitalisation will lead to the death of the textbook. Up to now, however, we have assumed that the relationship between on-line and print-based publishing is simply one of competition. In fact, as demonstrated by the case studies below, the relationship is more complex.

David Friedman

As we saw above, David Friedman is the author of *Price Theory*, a book that was published first in printed form and then on the internet. Note the interaction between print and electronic publication. Samuel Cameron may ask why students would buy a microeconomic textbook when they can download this one free, but one might equally well ask why Friedman, or any other author, would go to the trouble of writing such a book if he had not had the opportunity to publish the book commercially – on paper.

Friedman's website refers to another of his books, *Hidden Order*. Here too there is an interplay between electronic and print media, but of a different sort. The website offers access to a sample chapter, but not to the whole book. It also offers links to two on-line bookstores where the books can be ordered. In addition Friedman has posted a list of errata found in the printed book. Here we can see what is at the moment the most conventional form of interplay between the two media: the printed book remains the main product and the website markets the product, adds to it and updates it. The benefits of this form of interplay are obvious (not least that it usually involves the author in very little work beyond writing the book) but limited.

The website also features Friedman's latest book, *Law's Order*. Here the interplay is more adventurous. The book was printed by Princeton University Press. The website carries images of the entire text. The 'print' is small and not easy to read for any length of time. There is a copyright notice forbidding reproduction of the text and informing us that 'users are not permitted to mount this file on any network servers'. The website edition carries additional material (footnotes and web links) which Friedman says 'gets in the way of simply reading the book' itself. He invites users to suggest further web links.

The assumption underlying this web page is that readers will want to buy the printed version of *Law's Order* because it is the most readable, and portable, form. The exclusion of the footnotes from the printed book makes it less expensive to produce. The website adds extensively to the book and, through the provision of web links, keeps it up to date. Here the benefits of the interplay between website and printed book are greater, but so too is the work required from the author.

Gutenberg-e

Gutenberg-e is a project established by an eminent historian, Robert Darnton, along with Columbia University Press to enable scholars to publish books on-line. Although the project deals only with monographs, there are obvious comparisons to be made with the possibilities for textbooks.

Some of the Gutenberg-e monographs will read exactly like printed texts – indeed part of the project involves simply publishing on-line the text of monographs already printed. There will, however, be some monographs that work in ways that print cannot rival. A monograph on social history, for example, could enable the user to listen to songs referred to in the text, click on maps in technicolour that show the places featured in the discussion, or access the archive material that the scholar has analysed.

Again there is an interplay between electronic text and the printed word. Note that it was a traditional publisher that Darnton worked with to establish the project: the quality brand name is provided by an organisation that has established its reputation through the printed word. An important part of the deal that the project offers to authors is the right to publish their work in print three years after publication on-line. And, of course, the very name of the project symbolises continuity with print.

The McGraw-Hill Psycafe website

McGraw-Hill is a leading textbook publisher. One of their strengths is their psychology list. This list is accompanied by a website known as Psycafe. The site supports the printed text-books in what has fast become the conventional way. That is, it allows potential purchasers to scan content, read chapter summaries and download sample chapters.

However, the site also supports the books in more adventurous ways. There are services to students ranging from entertaining but fairly trivial features (quizzes and crosswords) to more serious forms of support (test-yourself pages and web links to psychology sites). For lecturers there are features that make the delivery of courses easier (powerpoint slides and class activities) as well as discussion groups and a page for exchanging teaching ideas.

Framing the whole site is the coffee-house concept that gives the site its title. The site's home page features a photograph of the interior of a café (though, rather disconcertingly, a deserted one) and presents the site as a 'virtual coffee house'. This creates something of the ambience provided by cafés in Borders' bookstores: books are associated with civilised, relaxed, living and reading becomes a less solitary activity. The concept informs the design of the site as a whole. The message to the user might be summarised as 'Relax! McGraw-Hill can make learning easier and more entertaining for you – and whether you are a student or academic, you needn't feel alone in your work'. Buying a McGraw-Hill textbook comes to feel like joining a club.

This type of website challenges Sven Birketts' negative responses to the internet. The tasteful graphics and spacious design give the site little of the 'ungainliness' that, according to Birketts, characterises the internet. Most importantly, the website complements printed books rather than competing against them. Without a copy of one of McGraw-Hill's textbooks in front of you, the site is of little use: with a copy, the site adds value for all concerned.

The internet and the printed word: a synthesis of views

The case studies above show that the relationship between on-line publishing and print is not static, nor is it simply a question of either/or. There are numerous forms of interplay between the two media, including many in which the two forms of publishing complement each other.

Overall, there are four main ways in which the internet can complement paper textbook publishing. First, it increases the total market. It does this by enabling college courses to be offered to students on-line. This allows students to enrol who otherwise, for reasons of time, location or money, would not be able to.

Second, through publishers' and retailers' websites the internet offers a sales and marketing channel. Admittedly, the effects of this on the textbook industry as a whole are equivocal. Large internet retailers use their market share to negotiate larger discounts with publishers, thereby reducing the income available to publishers and authors. Moreover, many sales of books on the internet merely substitute for sales from bricks and mortar. However, by making textbooks more attractive (through supporting websites) and easier to buy, the internet should increase the textbook market as a whole.

Third, the internet, along with other aspects of computing, has become a subject for textbook authors to write about. The simplest answer to anyone who believes that the internet will kill the printed word is to take them into a bookstore and show them the burgeoning section on computing. Admittedly, many of these books are not textbooks – but some are: I am not the only editor in charge of a list of computer studies textbooks.

Fourth, as we have seen from the case studies above, the internet enables publishers and authors to supplement textbooks with websites, thereby making them more extensive, easier to use and more up to date.

A view of the future

As a prospective author of textbooks, you will want to know not only how the internet is affecting the industry now but also how it will do so in the future. Nobody knows, of course, but on the basis of existing trends and an understanding of the logic behind them it is possible to make some educated guesses.

Here, then, is my short-term forecast:

1. It will become de rigueur to support textbooks with websites. At the moment, the situation is patchy, but the clear trend is towards supplementing textbooks with sample chapters, tables of contents, updates and web links on the internet. Publishers who don't do this, at least for major projects, are already beginning to look anachronistic.
2. By changing the way we read, think and compose, the internet will change the structure of textbooks. The recognition of alternative reading paths, the design features of *The English Studies Book* that we discussed in Chapter 5 (the provision of notes and references at the end of passages rather than chapters, for example), and the provision of alternative tables of contents will all become standard.
3. There will be two classes of textbook: (a) books for which website support, hyperlinks and so on, remain supplementary – with these books the electronic features will provide additional benefits, but there will be no need for the reader to use them: the printed book will still work as a free-standing product – and (b) books that form part of multimedia products to which the electronic features are integral. The advantage of multimedia products is that each chunk of information can be conveyed in the medium best suited to it (for example, in a film studies product, the theoretical discussion might be on paper and the examples on video clips). The disadvantage is that the books no longer work as free-standing products and readers will be obliged to access electronic data.
4. Increasingly, books will become available in dual format, i.e. both in printed form and as e-books. The decision to publish in both formats will seem no more innovative than the decision to publish the printed book in both hard and soft covers.

5. Customers will be able to choose between either buying a book as a whole or, through micropayments, buying parts of it.

6. For publishers there will be a premium on branding as a guarantee of quality assurance. The development of electronic publishing sometimes excites authors who believe that it offers a way of by-passing the publisher. But although it may be easy to produce electronic text, why would anyone decide to buy or read it if it isn't produced by a reputable publisher? In fact, nothing much has altered: authors have long been able to self-publish in print, but very few do and even fewer succeed. What is possible is that other relevant organisations will begin to use their brand names more to compete against publishers in the provision of electronic text. We saw above that one of Robert Darnton's on-line publishing projects relies on Columbia University Press for the branding: interestingly, another of his projects uses the American Council of Learned Societies as the brand.

Implications for authors

Finally, let us draw out the implications of all of this for authors. I have set these out in the order in which an author working on a book will encounter them.

1. The internet provides more to write about. This is true not only for authors working in computer studies and allied fields such as media studies, cultural studies and business studies. Few disciplines are unaffected. In *An Introduction to Counselling*, for example, John McLeod includes a discussion of counselling by e-mail.

2. In deciding which publisher to approach, you will need to give more weight to the question of how well placed each publisher is to exploit the potential of electronic text. Publishers' relationships with internet booksellers, the quality and extent of their own websites, and their experience of producing e-books and other electronic products are all becoming important indicators of their suitability to publish textbook projects.

3. When negotiating contracts, you will need to give more attention to the section on electronic rights. As I said in Chapter 3, this is not the place to consider the nitty-gritty of contracts, but let us consider some of the broader issues. Authors will need to consider whether it is clear which areas of electronic publishing and broadcasting are covered in the contract. Note that many publishers have not revised their standard contracts for many years and so the contracts may well not be appropriate. Authors will also want to consider whether the publisher is in a position to exploit electronic rights: if not, the author might seek to withhold those rights and sell them to a third party. The rate of payment on offer for electronic rights is also important and authors will want, at the very least, an explanation from the publisher of the thinking behind the offer. They will want to consider how much extra work is implied in the contract and whether that amount is defined. (If you commit to helping your publisher to maintain a website, how much work will that involve? And do you really want to keep working on that project years after publication?) To the extent that such work increases sales, the prospect of extra royalty payments provides an incentive, but if the publisher can demand extra work with no extra payment in advance, the risk is being carried wholly by the author. It is entirely possible to work industriously on producing an impressive web page for a book only to find that it has negligible impact on sales.

4. The concept of a chapter will change. As all of us (readers and writers) become less practised at working with sustained arguments and increasingly habituated to short passages, chapters will become shorter or authors will dispense with the concept of chapters (as Rob Pope did in *The English Studies Book*) and think in terms of short, numbered, passages instead.

5. Writing will be made easier by the development of software. Most of the writers' software developed so far has been designed for authors of fiction and film scripts, but there is already some software that might help textbook authors. For example, there is MindManager™ (designed to help with thinking and planning) and ProCite™ (for help with references).

161

6. As projects become more driven by multimedia, authors will become team players even more than they are today. Authors already work alongside editors, publishers' reviewers, designers and so on, but the design of projects that are multimedia from inception involves authors becoming team players from Day 1.
7. The nature of the author's work after publication will also change. Where a print-based book is accompanied by a website, authors will be encouraged to provide updates between editions. Where a book is published as an e-book, authors will be encouraged to help the publisher update the text constantly.

Coda

In all the discussion of the impact of technology on textbooks, we should not forget that the textbook itself is a kind of technology – one that has been around rather longer than most other kinds (according to the OED, the term has existed with its current meaning since 1779). In order of importance it might not rank quite as high as the wheel, say, or the clock yet by no stretch of the imagination is it unimportant. It supports good teaching, offsets bad teaching, facilitates work on assignments and revision out of class, and enables independent study. To assess its importance, consider the following questions:

- How would the history of education and the professions be different without the textbook?
- How sustainable would our current systems of education and training be without textbooks?
- Without the contribution of textbooks to the diffusion of knowledge and the development of education, could such forms of technology as CD-ROMs, the internet and e-books ever have been developed?

Compared to other media and other forms of publishing, textbooks sometimes suffer from a lack of glamour and, in academic circles preoccupied by research, they lack kudos, yet nobody doubts that they play an essential role in modern life.

I have never had any particular aptitude for history. When I was thirteen, I finished the first term of the academic year placed 21st in my class for that subject. In the second term I finished 23rd. In the third term I decided to read the class textbook from cover to cover and finished third. If you write a successful textbook, you can make an important contribution to the knowledge and understanding of thousands of people. And you get the royalties.

Appendix: A Sample Book Proposal

The following is a proposal sent to Continuum by Yvonne Hillier. The proposal followed a one and a half hour discussion with the editor a few days beforehand.

Reflective Teaching for Learning in Adult and Further Education

'Understanding precedes action' (Lawson, 1998)

This book is aimed at anyone who is involved in working with adult learners. It is primarily intended to enable those who are fairly new to the field to develop practice which is informed both by formal theory and through an ongoing process of critical reflection. It draws upon the author's twenty years' experience of working with adults across a range of contexts including basic skills, tutor training, volunteer training, students studying at masters level and developing university teaching and learning practices. A fundamental theme underpinning the book is that people develop theories about their daily practice which are not usually explicit but which continually inform what they do. Practitioners will be encouraged to question and challenge what they do to solve the problems and challenges facing them as they enable adults to learn in a fast changing social and political context.

The book will assist practitioners working towards accredited professional development, in particular the City and Guilds 7306/3 Teaching Certificate, Certificate in Education awards. It will support those who are developing programmes to meet the new Further Education National Training Organisation (FENTO) standards.

Contents

SECTION I: POLICY AND THEORY

Introduction
This section will commence with a case study outlining the typical challenges encountered when working with adult learners. The example will establish the need to adopt a problem-solving approach to adult learning which will rely upon practitioners thinking and reflecting critically on what they currently do and then drawing upon theories and practices which are in the public domain.

The rationale for the book is identifying that insights, not solutions, help professional development. It is based on an empowering notion that practitioners have a wealth of tacit knowledge developed through personal experience and interaction with others. This knowledge needs to be both recognised and further developed.

In each chapter an issue will be raised in the form of a question. This will be followed by a discussion of current theory and practice, taking account of possible contexts including traditional face-to-face, distance- and web-based learning. The chapters will particularly address underpinning approaches to inclusive learning and equal opportunities, rather than discuss these as separate issues.

Chapter 1: Policy in lifelong learning: adults and their learning
This chapter will set the scene of current adult learning contexts. It will address the following areas:

- Lifelong learning agenda
- Formal and informal learning
- Accreditation of learning
- Professionalisation of adult teaching
- Guidance
- Technology

Chapter 2: Reflective practice in adult learning
This chapter will develop the rationale for the book through

discussing how reflective practice has developed from its philosophical and social theory roots. It will include analysis of:

- Theoretical origins – critical theory
- Application to the field of adult learning
- Process of reflective practice
- Tacit versus explicit knowledge

SECTION II: PROFESSIONAL KNOWLEDGE
The following chapters are based upon the areas covered by
teaching awards. In each chapter, examples will be used to
illustrate current practice and challenges for the practitioner.
All will start with a question to be examined.

Chapter 3: Deciding what to teach

- Identification of learning styles
- Identification of aims and objectives
- Individual and group requirements
- Educational guidance

Chapter 4: Developing learning resources

- Using traditional resources
- Using technology
- Catering for individual and group requirements

Chapter 5: Structuring a learning programme

- Developing aims and objectives for a learning programme
- Teaching and learning methods
- Flexible learning

Chapter 6: Working with groups

- Group dynamics
- Working with mixed level groups
- Working with groups on-line

Chapter 7: Assessing learning

- Formative assessment
- Summative assessment
- Self and peer assessment
- Meeting awarding body requirements

Chapter 8: Evaluating learning programmes

- Why evaluate?
- Identifying stakeholders
- Ways and means
- Accountability: LSC criteria, OFSTED/FEFC/Quality assurance

Chapter 9: Improving professional practice

- Identification of personal development requirements
- Ways and means
- Reflective practice for professional development
- Networking with colleagues
- Accreditation of professional development

Length

It is quite daunting for practitioners to wade through a large tome. This book will aim to be succinct and accessible. It is unlikely to total more than 80 000 words.

Intended markets

The primary market will be tutors and trainers in adult and further education who are working towards accredited professional development in the UK. With the introduction of FENTO all staff in Further Education (FE) will require an initial teaching qualification and need to demonstrate ongoing professional development. The majority of learners in FE are adults and therefore the need to address good practice in adult learning is extensive. The proposed Learning and Skills Council will have responsibility for all post-compulsory education excluding higher education. There will be two inspectorates, one primarily responsible for adult learners. These initiatives will re-enforce demand for good practice and professional accreditation of staff in FE.

There are about 550 FE colleges in the UK and a further 50+ tertiary colleges. There are approximately 70 000 academic staff working in FE colleges.

Most Certificate in Education programmes address differing needs of learners and it is anticipated that the book will therefore be of interest to students studying at postgraduate level.

Finally, continuing professional development for practitioners in adult learning follows similar patterns in Australia, New Zealand and the US and Canada. European initiatives in developing approaches to adult learning through Socrates and Leonardo programmes may provide further interest in markets closer to the UK.

The book will address generic issues of teaching and learning and therefore appeal to the markets mentioned above. As adult learning in the UK has to address multicultural issues to reflect the society in which it is located, the case studies and examples will therefore take account of the particular demands of local, regional and national groups in the UK. The cases should have enough transferability to the wider markets.

Competition

There are a number of books addressing adult learning. The most popular is Minton's *Teaching Skills in Further and Adult Education*, ranked 3,704 on amazon.co.uk (Feb 2000). Other texts include Rogers' *Adult Learning* which is highly popular amongst course leaders at Cert Ed and City and Guilds level. Rogers' book was written initially for the adult education market. The proposed book is the only one which includes reflective practice in its title and which attempts to take a more proactive approach in addressing issues in learning.

Author details

Dr Yvonne Hillier, BSc, PGCE, Med, PhD, FRSA
Papers, articles and books
[Yvonne lists a dozen texts that she has written for publications such as *Adult Education* and *Higher Education Review*.]
Conference papers
[Yvonne lists half a dozen papers given to conferences such as the International Conference on Training Adult Educators and the annual conference of the Society for Research in Higher Education (SRHE).]
Article Reviews and Reviews
[Yvonne lists nine reviews published in *Higher Education Review*.]

Yvonne Hillier is the co-ordinator of the Further Education Research Network for London and South East and a member of the planning group of the annual conference, supported by FEDA. She attends the SRHE annual conference and has presented a paper at this conference in 1999 on work-based learning in France and the UK. She is an external verifier for the City and Guilds 7306/7, 7281 and 9281 awards in training and development. She is a member of the course board for the City Lit's PGCE validated by the City University. She has just developed the first Certificate in teaching and learning at City University and is currently developing a Diploma in Education for university staff.

The author wishes to write a book that both celebrates and acknowledges the wealth of tacit knowledge held by practitioners in the field of learning and develops a critical approach to this practice. It will build upon the experience gathered from a range of teaching practices in adult learning and will contribute to the research culture in the Department of Continuing Education, City University, where the author is based.

Submission

It is hoped to submit a manuscript by August 2001.

Illustrations

It is anticipated that examples of resources, diagrams, web pages and other illustrations will be included in the book. Not all of these will be camera-ready, but advice is sought from Continuum on this matter.

Benefits to readers

Readers will be able to identify their own practice and knowledge of adult learning. They will be able to recognise where they can further develop their practice and knowledge. They will be able to work towards accreditation of their professional practice as a result of reading the book and working on examples and case studies.

Contact details

[name, postal address, home and work telephone and fax numbers, and e-mail address provided]

The proposal was successful and a contract authorised for the book to be published in 2002.

Notes

A list of the website addresses mentioned in these notes appears on the A & C Black website at **www.textbookwriter.com**.

Chapter 1

Guidance on the use of information technology can be found in *The Internet: A Writer's Guide* by Jane Dorner. The book also lists websites that provide IT guidance. The BBC's website (**www.bbc.co.uk/webwise**) is particularly useful for guidance about the internet and Oxford University Press's website (**www.oucs.ox.ac.uk/documentation/leaflets/L03.html**) offers guidance concerning e-mail.

Practical advice on time management in general is provided by Edwin C. Bliss, *Getting Things Done*. For advice on time management directed specifically to writers, including an account of freewriting, see the first few chapters of the second edition of Joseph M. Moxley and Todd Taylor (eds), *Writing and Publishing for Academic Authors*.

A general book on project management is Celia Burton and Norma Michael, *A Practical Guide to Project Management*. Ways of using publication as a stepping stone to other ways of earning income are explained in Michael H. Sedge, *Marketing Strategies for Writing*.

Chapter 2

Research for Writers by Ann Hoffmann is invaluable. Unlike many such books, it considers the needs of non-fiction writers as well as novelists.

Digests of courses in the UK are available on the internet on the UCAS website (**www.ucas.ac.uk**) and ECCTIS website (**www.ecctis.co.uk**). Details of the National Curriculum are available on the Qualifications and Curriculum Authority's website (**www.qca.org.uk**). Digests in book form include the *CRAC Degree Course Guide*. Guides to college courses in the US are published in Barron's Educational Series. Details of university courses in the UK are available on Pearson's website (**www.awl-he.com/sites.html**) and in the US at **www.aacu-edu.org/ membership/list.html**.

Reports of school inspections in the UK are available on the internet at **www.ofsted.gov.uk**. Journals reporting empirical research into pedagogic trends include the *British Journal of In-Service Education, Teachers and Teaching: Theory and Practice* and *Teaching in Higher Education*. Book-length studies include *Promoting Quality in Learning, What Pupils Say* and *What Teachers Do*. Details of subject associations and their journals in the UK are given in *The Education Yearbook*, which is published annually.

Website addresses for bookstores and publishers are available on the internet at **www.bookweb.co.uk** and **www.library.vander bilt.edu/law/acqs/pubr.html**. Price-browsers are available at **www.evenbetter.com** and **www.bookbrain.co.uk**. Sites for buying second-hand include **www.bibliofind.com** and **www.thoemmes-antiquarian.com**.

Three websites to help you evaluate the websites that you use in research are: Evaluating Internet Research Sources, **www.vanguard.edu/library/www/eval.htm**; Evaluating Information found on the Net, **http://milton.mse.jhu.edu/research/ education/net.html**; and, my favourite, Internet Detective, **www.sosig.ac.uk/desire/internet-detective.html**.

Chapter 3

Barry Turner, *The Writer's Handbook* and the website at **www.library.vanderbilt.edu/law/acqs/pubr.html** allow you to search for publishers by subject.

Advice on the question of co-authorship is provided in Ch. 12 of Joseph M. Moxley and Todd Taylor (eds), *Writing and Publishing for Academic Authors*. Further examples of book proposals may be found in Jeff Herman and Deborah M. Adams, *Write the Perfect Book Proposal: 10 proposals that sold and why*. An introduction to publishing contracts is provided by Michael Legat, *An Author's Guide to Publishing*. In the UK the Society of Authors provides its members with clause-by-clause guidance on contracts (**www.writers.org.uk/society**). Carole Blake, *From Pitch to Publication* provides detailed advice on negotiating and working with publishers from proposal stage onwards.

Chapter 4

David Kolb's theory of learning styles is explained in *Experiential Learning*.

Chapter 5

The quotation from Nik Chmiel is from an article entitled 'You really must meet...', which appeared on p. 34 of the *THES* on 7 May 1999. Jim Cummins' thinking is explained in Tony Cline and Norah Frederickson (eds), *Curriculum Related Assessment, Cummins and Bilingual Children*. Kieran Egan's theory of instruction is explained in *Teaching as Story Telling*. The quotations from Todd Gitlin are from pp. 20–21 of *The Twilight of Common Dreams*.

Chapter 6

The passage beginning 'When Ulysses S. Grant...' is quoted on p. 41 of *Cultural Literacy: What every American needs to know*. The discussion by E. D. Hirsch of that passage, cited above, is on p. 54 of that book.

Chapter 7

The Quiller-Couch passage is from pp. 650–51 of the *New Oxford Book of English Prose*.

Etymological resources include: Mary Byrne, *Eureka!*; C. T. Onions, *The Oxford Dictionary of Etymology*; and John Ayto, *Bloomsbury Dictionary of Word Origins*. Detailed advice on non-sexist approaches to the pronoun problem and on much else is given in *The Handbook of Non-Sexist Writing* by Casey Miller and Kate Swift. Guidance on using the English language is provided by the Plain English Campaign on **www.plainenglishcampaign.com**.

Chapter 8

The first quotation from Howard Becker is from p. 13 and the second from pp. 78–79.

An authoritative writers' dictionary is the *Oxford Writers' Dictionary*. *The King's English* is on-line at **www.columbia.edu/ acis/bartleby/fowler**. Specialist reference books include B. A. Phythian, *A Concise Dictionary of Confusables* and Bill Bryson, *Penguin Dictionary of Troublesome Words*.

A worked example of bottom-up redrafting is given by Howard Becker on pp. 74–77.

Chapter 9

For a fuller discussion of diagrams, see Malcolm Craig, *Thinking Visually*. For an exploration of the application of the language of the senses, see Sue Knight, *NLP at Work*.

Chapter 10

Hans Wellisch, *Indexing from A to Z* includes essays on exhaustivity and specificity. The alphabetical example involving South Australia etc. is taken from G. Norman Knight, *Indexing, The Art of*.

Chapter 11

For advice on marketing, see Alison Baverstock, *How to Market Books*. For advice on using the media, see Martin Tierney, *The Media and How to Use It*.

The source for the Asa Briggs quotation is 'History that improves with age' (*THES*, 25 February 2000). The quotation from John Driffill is from 'A dime for your sterling thoughts' (*THES*, 26 May 2000).

Chapter 12

The quotation from Samuel Cameron is from 'Oprah meets a grizzly' in the Textbook Guide in the *THES* (26 May 2000). David Friedman's website address is **www.best.com/~ddfr/**. The research by the Council for Academic and Professional Publishers is reported in *The Bookseller* (21 August 2000). For a discussion of micropayments, see 'The case for micropayments' by Jakob Nielsen at **www.useit.com/alertbox/980125.html**. A report on the Gutenberg-e project is available from Inside Publishing on-line at **www.linguafranca.com/0007/inside-webcast.html**. The website address for McGraw-Hill's Psycafe is **www.mhhe.com/socscience/ intro/cafe/psycafm.htm**. An evaluation by Silvia Bartolic-Zlomislic and A. W. Bates of on-line courses is available at **http:/bates.cstudies.ubc.ca/investing.html**. To find out more about ProCite™, go to **www.isinet.com/products/refman.html**; for MindManager™, go to **www.mindman.co.uk**.

Further reading

Marilyn Chambliss and Robert Calfee, *Textbooks for Learning* provides an in-depth, heavyweight, study of the textbook genre and industry. For further discussion of the practice and theory of writing, see Frank Smith, *Writing and the Writer*.

Books Mentioned in the Text

Action Research in Higher Education: Examples and reflections, Ortrun Zuber-Skerritt, Kogan Page, 1992

Advanced Business Studies through Diagrams, Andrew Gillespie, Oxford University Press, 1998 (2nd edn.)

The Age of Improvement, 1783–1867, Asa Briggs, Longman, 2000 (2nd edn.; 1st edn. 1959)

An Author's Guide to Publishing, Michael Legat, Robert Hale, 1998 (3rd edn.)

Basic Economics, Arnold Heertje and Brian R. G. Robinson, Holt, Rinehart & Winston, 1982 (Revised 1st edn.)

Basic Marketing: Principles and Practice, Tom Cannon, Cassell, 1996 (4th edn.)

Becoming a Writer: The classic inspirational guide, Dorothea Brande, Papermac, 1983

Bloomsbury Dictionary of Word Origins, John Ayto, Bloomsbury, 1991

Bloomsbury Good Word Guide, Martin H. Manser (ed.), Bloomsbury, 1988

Books in Print, RR Bowker

Chambers Dictionary of Foreign Words and Phrases, Rosalind Ferguson, Chambers, 1995

The Complete Plain Words, Sir Ernest Gowers, Penguin, 1997

Comprehension Success, James Driver, Oxford University Press, 1998

A Concise Dictionary of Confusables, B. A. Phythian, Hodder & Stoughton, 1989

CRAC Degree Course Guide, Trotman, published annually

Creating Texts: An introduction to the study of composition, Walter Nash and David Stacey, Longman, 1997

Cultural Literacy: What every American needs to know, E. D. Hirsch, Houghton Mifflin, 1987

Curriculum Related Assessment, Cummins and Bilingual Children, Tony Cline and Norah Frederickson (eds), Multilingual Matters, 1996

Economics, Joseph Stiglitz, W.W. Norton, 1997

Economics, Joseph Stiglitz and John Driffill, W.W. Norton, 2000

The Education Yearbook, Financial Times, annually

The English Studies Book, Rob Pope, Routledge, 1998

Essential GCSE English for Mature Students, Diana Wallsgrove, Collins Educational, 1994

Eureka!: A dictionary of Latin and Greek elements in English words, Mary Byrne, David & Charles, 1987

Experiential Learning: Experience as the source of learning and development, David A. Kolb, Prentice Hall, 1984

From Pitch to Publication, Carole Blake, Pan, 1999

Geography: A modern synthesis, Peter Haggett, Harper & Row, 1979 (3rd international edn.)

Getting Things Done, Edwin C. Bliss, Bantam Books, 1977

Good Practice in Childcare, Janet Kay, Continuum, 2001

The Gutenberg Elegies: The fate of reading in an electronic age, Sven Birketts, Faber & Faber, 1994

Handbook of Non-Sexist Writing for Writers, Editors and Speakers, Casey Miller and Kate Swift, Women's Press, 1995

Hidden Order: The economics of everyday life, David Friedman, HarperCollins, 1997

How Exams Really Work, J. G. Lloyd, Cassell, 1999

How to Market Books, Alison Baverstock, Kogan Page, 1999

Indexing from A to Z, Hans H. Wellisch, The H. W. Wilson Company, 1991

Indexing, The Art of: A guide to the indexing of books and periodicals, G. Norman Knight, George Allen & Unwin, 1979

The Internet: A Writer's Guide, Jane Dorner, A & C Black, 2000

An Introduction to Children's Literature, Peter Hunt, Oxford University Press, 1994

An Introduction to Counselling, John McLeod, Open University Press, 1998 (2nd edn.)

Introduction to English Language, N. F. Blake and Jean Moorhead, Macmillan, 1993

Books mentioned in the text

An Introduction to a Mathematical Treatment of Economics, G. C. Archibald & Richard G. Lipsey, Weidenfeld & Nicolson, 1977 (3rd edn.)

Introduction to Positive Economics, Richard G. Lipsey, Weidenfeld & Nicolson, 1983 (6th edn.)

Key Issues in Education and Teaching, John Wilson, Cassell, 2000

The King's English: The classic guide to written English, H. W. Fowler & F. G. Fowler, Oxford University Press, 1973 (3rd edn.)

Law's Order, David Friedman, Princeton University Press, 2000

Literary Systematics, Helmut Bonheim, D.S. Brewer, 1990

Literature for Democracy: Reading as a social act, Gordon M. Pradl, Boynton/Cook, 1996

Marketing Strategies for Writing, Michael H. Sedge, Allworth, 1999

The Media and How to Use It, Martin Tierney, Veritas, 1985

Modern Drama in Theory and Practice: vol. 1, J. L. Styan, Cambridge University Press, 1983

The New Oxford Book of English Prose, John Gross (ed.), Oxford University Press, 1998

NLP at Work: the difference that makes a difference at work, Sue Knight, Nicholas Brealey, 1996

The Oxford Dictionary of English Etymology, C. T. Onions (ed.), Oxford University Press, 1966

Oxford Writers' Dictionary, R.E. Allen (ed.), Oxford University Press, 1990

Penguin Dictionary of Troublesome Words, Bill Bryson, Allen Lane, 1984

A Practical Guide to Project Management, Celia Burton and Norma Michael, Kogan Page, 1992

Price Theory: An intermediate text, David Friedman, South-Western, 1992

Principles of Business for CXC: with multiple choice questions, Dr Sam Seunarine, Continuum (4th edn.)

Promoting Quality in Learning: Does England have the answer?, Patricia Broadfoot et al., Cassell, 2000

Reflective Teaching, Andrew Pollard, Continuum, forthcoming

Reflective Teaching in the Primary School, Andrew Pollard, Cassell, 1996 (3rd edn.)

Research for Writers, Ann Hoffmann, A & C Black, 1999 (6th edn.)

Sociology: Themes and perspectives, Michael Haralambos and Martin Holborn, Collins Educational, 1995

Stress in Young People: What's new and what to do, Sarah McNamara, Continuum, 2001

Teaching as Story Telling: An alternative approach to teaching and the curriculum, Kieran Egan, Routledge, 1988

Teaching in Further Education, L. B. Curzon, Cassell, 1997 (5th edn.)

Textbooks for Learning: Nurturing Children's Minds, Marilyn J. Chambliss and Robert C. Calfee, Blackwell, 1998

Thinking Visually: Business applications of fourteen core diagrams, Malcolm Craig, Continuum, 2000

The Twilight of Common Dreams: Why America is wracked by culture wars, Todd Gitlin, Metropolitan Books, 1995

Understanding Literature, Robin Mayhead, Cambridge University Press, 1965

Usage and Abusage: A guide to good English, Eric Partridge and Janet Whitcut (ed.), Penguin, 1999

Whatever Happened to Britain? The economics of decline, John Eatwell, Duckworth, 1982

What Pupils Say: Changing policy and practice in primary education, Andrew Pollard et al., Continuum, 2000

What Teachers Do: Changing policy and practice in primary education, Marilyn Osborn et al., Continuum, 2000

Whitaker's Books in Print, Whitaker, published annually electronically

Write the Perfect Book Proposal: 10 proposals that sold and why, Jeff Herman & Deborah M. Adams, John Wiley & Sons, 1993

Writers' and Artists' Yearbook, A & C Black, published annually

The Writer's Handbook, Barry Turner, Pan, 2000

Writing and Publishing for Academic Authors, Joseph M. Moxley and Todd Taylor (eds), Rowman and Littlefield, 1977

Writing for Social Scientists: How to start and finish your thesis, book or article, Howard S. Becker, University of Chicago Press, 1986

Writing and the Writer, Frank Smith, Heinemann Educational, 1982

Index